I am two!

Working effectively with two year olds and their families

Kay Mathieson

ISBN-10   0-904187-60-8

ISBN-13   978-0-904187-60-1

EAN   9780904187601

Published by:

The British Association for Early Childhood Education

136 Cavell Street, London, E1 2JA

Telephone: + 44 207 539 5400

Fax: + 44 207 539 5409

Email: office@early-education.org.uk

Website   www.early-education.org.uk

Charity registered in England and Wales no. 313082
Charity registered in Scotland no. SC039472
A company limited by guarantee registered in England no 395548

Contents

I am two!

Introduction

About this book

To spend time in the company of a two year old is to be given the opportunity to discover the world as if for the first time. Taking time to feel the excitement of shared discovery and exploration creates opportunities for meaningful thinking and emotional connection.

This book sets out to explore some of the challenges and delights of working with two year olds in the context of early years provision. The phrase 'two year olds' is used throughout the book but is not intended to be taken literally — experiencing these significant changes in development can begin before the child's first birthday and continue well beyond their third. The essence of being two is about major changes in brain development, gaining a sense of self as an individual, beginning to use language in social contexts and also in thinking and having the physical ability to move independently and with increasing control.

It is also not possible to look at 'twoness' in complete isolation. At two, a child already has their own unique story. This story gives many insights about why they are where they are in their thinking, learning and view of the world. For this reason, included in this book are some brief explorations of children's earlier developments, as well as the significant social networks and their relationships with a range of peers and other adults that will have been established. In order to gain insight into why the child may be making sense of the world in particular way, it is important to consider their story to date as a context for their learning.

The book is organised into three sections: early development, the relationship between parents and practitioners and finally the importance of thinking about early intervention and the positive impact this can have, especially for our two year olds.

The references and resources cited have been deliberately chosen to offer a range of sources for further reading and developing interest, at a variety of levels from introductory to more experienced.

Early development

This section gives a brief overview of some significant aspects of development leading up to the two year old phase. The intention is to give a flavour of the way in which later developments are influenced by earlier experiences and progress. The rapid brain development that takes place during the first two years makes this a very exciting but also very vulnerable time in a child's life.

Parents and practitioners

While this book draws significantly on the requirements of the Early Years Foundation Stage (EYFS) in England, the importance of engaging with parents, particularly vulnerable families, is a core message in all the UK early years frameworks. From the individual child's perspective it is a crucial element to support their learning and understanding. Parental experience, understanding and confidence vary over time and in response to many things. Conversations with parents often highlight anxieties and concerns about the behaviour of their two year olds. Practitioners are ideally placed to engage positively with parents and to co-construct ways of understanding and responding to an individual two year old's behaviour. Although seldom an easy task, the benefits for the child and parent can be transforming.

Developing positive relationships with parents and collaborating to support individual children is a very rewarding aspect of working in early years provision. Establishing a solid relationship with parents will, to a greater extent, determine whether the relationship will be a positive, supportive experience, or a more complex and difficult one. All sorts of preconceived ideas on both sides of the relationship can colour these early interactions and it is the professional responsibility of the practitioners to make every effort to build a positive and supportive rapport with all parents and families. In doing so we can offer much more effective support for the children in our care.

Inevitably there will be times when some of these relationships are less secure than others. As professionals we need to lay aside our personal feelings and focus on the need to recognise the difference these relationships can make to individual children and their families. Keeping the lines of communication open and continuing to be proactive in developing the relationship, even through difficult times, is what really makes the difference to the lives of families.

Early intervention

In society, the patterns and expectations around family life change continually.[1] We are currently in a time when the majority of children attend some form of early years provision before they attend school. Government policy inevitably impacts on our professional understanding and the early years sector has been a high priority for several years now.[2] Currently in the UK, a major priority is to improve the health and wellbeing of our children.[3] Giving our youngest children a good start in life is now recognised as a significant investment that will reduce the incidence and cost of later problems.[4] Health, education and social care services are focusing on improving diet, exercise, family health, general wellbeing and reducing poverty. The impact for early brain development of early risk factors, particularly those associated with poverty, is significant, so much so that some three year olds can already be nine months behind in learning and development in comparison with peers who have had a more positive start to life.[5] Access to high quality early years provision has the potential to make a real difference to the life experience of all young children and their families, but especially those at risk. This gives us a chance to reconsider what high quality provision for our two year olds might look like, and why it is so important.

Usually, the focus of a parent's enquiry is related to their own child. The reassurance that your child is developing in expected ways, being understood, able to do things similar to their peer group, being treated fairly, liked and cared for by practitioners, is something we constantly seek as parents. As practitioners, we are in a position to support all parents by bringing together our knowledge of child development, effective practice and the needs of their individual child.

Recent research supports the view that intervening early in a child's life or when a difficulty is first recognised, is more cost effective and has greater benefits than when a child is older, or a problem more entrenched.[6] The phrase 'early intervention' can feel like a complex and technical process. In reality, it is more about doing 'what we know matters' really well. Using our developing knowledge of individual children with their families from the beginning of our relationship, creates a context in which we can all be alert to concerns as well as a range of ways in which these concerns

can be explored, alleviated or shared more widely as appropriate. Our ongoing evidence of children's development is an important part of this picture and provides others with a wider perspective to inform their judgments.

Being two – an introduction

'Twoness' is special because so much is happening during this time. Huge changes take place for children in their physical, social and thinking abilities. The speed of change is fantastic and the impact on day-to-day experience is quite incredible. That said, two year olds can get a lot of bad press as terms such as 'terrible twos' and 'two year old tantrums' attest. Being two is one of the most amazing, fascinating, confusing and unsettling developmental phases of a child's life.

By the age of two children already have significant social networks. Their relationships with a range of adults will influence their understanding of how the world works. These adults are all developing their own relationship with each individual two year old. To transform this social network into a support network the adults need to share and communicate their unique perspectives of the two year old. These adults may be parents, aunties, uncles, grandparents, family, friends, health professionals, social care professionals or early years practitioners.

This book is very much rooted in a social constructionist approach based on Vygotskian and Piagetian theories. This approach is complemented by exploration of current neuroscience and the implications for our understanding of child development. Taking this approach therefore brings together thinking about the importance of the relationships a child experiences and the ways in which these influence early learning and brain development. These relationships also take place in a wider social culture which informs parent and practitioner thinking about child rearing and developmental expectations of children.

A key point of this approach is that learning takes place in a social context and is a social process, and therefore relationships are integral to enabling effective learning. In particular the relationships with 'more experienced others' provides an opportunity for '**scaffolding**' the learning of those less experienced. The word 'scaffolding' was first applied in a learning context, to describe the process of a child solving a problem with assistance from an adult, that they would otherwise be unable to solve on their own.[7] In this context, the adult is able to control aspects of the task that are currently too difficult for the child. The adult is then able to support the child's understanding and/or physical skills to encourage the child's participation, engagement and success in completing the task.

A core element of 'scaffolding' is that it needs to build on what the child demonstrates that they already know or understand and extend their thinking to include new ideas, concepts and skills. The 'more experienced others' need not be adults but can equally be more experienced peers, therefore each child's thinking can be both scaffolded **by others** as well as providing scaffolding **for others** depending on the specific situation.

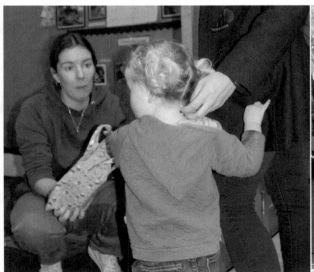

Chapter 1

Growing, growing, growing... the first two years

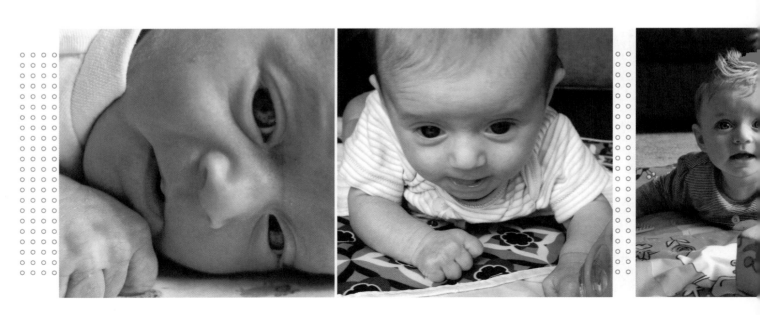

Harriet, (L to R):
10 days
10 weeks
6 months
8 months
11 months

Growing bodies

It is fairly obvious to say that during the first two years of life children grow at an astounding rate. Changes in size, shape and physical ability are dramatic and rapid during this early period.

Although physical growth follows a uniform pattern, there is significant variability in the timing of particular changes for individual children. For example, learning to walk can be acquired anytime from around nine to seventeen months.[8] Such variability is within normal range and not necessarily indicative of any delay or difficulty.

'Growing' for an infant and toddler is not just about getting taller and older but about the many systems in our bodies being established, linked together and coordinated with increasing precision and effectiveness. As each system grows it impacts on other bodily systems and extends what we can do and how well we can do it. For example, the separate and related development of the nervous system and muscles is a major factor in the development of the complex skill of walking.[9] However, this will also be significantly influenced by the environmental experiences[10] that our toddler is able to access.[11] It is increasingly understood just how important time spent in outdoor spaces is for all of our young children, to say nothing of the adults who work with them. Being outside feels different from being inside.[12] The freedom for bigger, faster, less controlled movement enables coordination and dexterity to increase along with the motivation to engage our interest and thinking in particular activities.[13] Playing alongside

two year olds allows us to encourage variety and extensions to their current abilities and thinking. In terms of movement this includes crawling, being cuddled, stretching, reaching and every other method of moving you can imagine. The wider the variety of opportunity the better, remembering too that periods of rest and relaxation, which can also be outside, are important for muscles and the nervous system to experience.

This complex process of development starts from conception and during the prenatal period the baby is already becoming aware of quiet and active times, regularly heard sounds, and changes in its mother's movement. This awareness is not a conscious thinking process because the baby's brain does not yet have this capacity, but these early sensations are still recognised by the baby after birth. For example, research shows that newborns recognise their mother's voice.[14] Sensory development is an integral part of prenatal and postnatal development. Around the 23rd week of pregnancy the baby is moving around and responding to both sounds and touch. By this stage the baby's major organs are formed, but they need to develop further before they are able to sustain breathing and blood flow outside the protective environment of the womb. Our understanding of these early developmental processes is still evolving, but it is clear that the prenatal experience is important and significant for the baby. This is a positive influence if the mother is able to have a healthy, nutritious and relatively stress free nine months. However family circumstances do not always enable this to be the case.

The birth itself will also impact on the baby's wellbeing. A relatively uncomplicated birth is likely to be more supportive to the baby's development than a traumatic difficult one. Again this is dependent on factors which are often beyond the control of the parents or supporting medical teams. Assuming all is well after birth the rapid process of physical growth continues in a predictable, but not exactly the same, way for each baby. At birth the baby's head is large relative to the rest of the body and the pattern of increasing physical control is seen to develop from 'head to toe', technically termed 'cephalo-caudal development.' As control of the head is gained the shoulder muscles and related nervous system connections enable the baby to raise their head and to refine movement control. This interconnected process has implications for controlling direction of vision that in turn will impact on early social responses.

In a similar manner the growth of the central nervous system enables development from the centre of the body outwards, known as proximodistal development. This allows control over trunk and neck movement before arms, hands and fingers. It also supports the healthy development and function of major bodily organs. In our work with young children this can be seen in the need to develop gross motor skills before fine motor skills can reach high levels of dexterity and fluency as needed for tasks such as handwriting.

A further important aspect of early physical development is turning over and twisting on the floor which helps children get a sense of their body and where it starts and ends as well as what it does. Physical movement is interconnected with other learning too. For example, reaching out, holding objects, showing curiosity and interest in the things around and being able to select things of interest. Being given time to explore again and again allows the baby to build up a sense of what the new thing is and does. At times this fascination includes parts of the body that suddenly seem to come into awareness, for example, children exploring their hands and feet, how they move and the extent to which their movement can be controlled.

These different aspects of development come together to allow coordinated movement. Crawling, shuffling, rolling, and tummy crawling are all important experiences in their own right and should not be seen as 'just a stage towards walking'. Each form of movement contributes in a range of ways towards standing unaided as well as building confidence in coordination, balance and muscle control. Independent exploration now becomes a prime objective for our two year olds, the whole world is there waiting for them to explore! This increasing coordination and movement control throughout the first two years, including standing upright, provides a whole new perspective on life. In particular, learning to stand upright and walk has major implications for social connection and independent choice of where you want to be and who you want to be with.[15]

Although these early developments progress significantly in the first two years of life, it is important to remember that the process continues beyond these early years as control and mastery of movement becomes refined and fluent.

The detailed complexity of all of these early developmental processes are still being explored and modern technology such as magnetic resonance imaging (MRI) and functional magnetic resonance imaging (fMRI) scanning have revolutionised our knowledge about how the body and brain work and develop.[16]

Growing brains

The early differentiation of cells in the development of the brain is an amazing process. The brain begins as a collection of cells that form the neural tube. From this basis different folds and structures are organised to form the various specialist areas of the brain. The basic structures of the brain and most of the required neurons are formed before birth. At birth an estimated 100 billion neurons are present in the brain, having been produced during rapid periods of growth, at times reaching 250,000 neurons per minute. As we know, this is just the beginning of the story. During the first two years the brain doubles its weight. This period of growth is not about increasing the number of neurons but establishing connections between them. This process includes **myelination**, which develops a sheath or covering around the axon of the neuron. The function of this covering is to improve the transmission of electrical signals making connections to other neurons, muscles or glands more effective.[17] While such rapid and dramatic changes during pregnancy and in early life are exciting, they also highlight the vulnerability of this period of life to a range of risk factors. Poor nutrition, restricted environments and negative relationships can all have a significant impact on the development of the brain during this period, with obvious longer term consequences.[18] It is important to note though that these early omissions can be alleviated, at least in part, through subsequent improvement in the experiences and opportunities for the child during this period too.

The early years of a child's development are a particularly important time because the nervous system is developing and has its highest level of plasticity. This means it is sensitive to changes in environmental conditions and has high levels of adaptability. Neuroscientists have also found evidence to suggest that there are sensitive periods for particular developments. This is not to say that if the development does not occur at this time it will never occur. But the nervous system goes through periods of intense growth when the access to an environment that provides critical sensory, movement and emotional experiences is particularly important. There are several sensitive periods that occur and contribute to the development of specific brain functions such as seeing and hearing. The last areas of the brain to be established are the frontal lobes. These areas are central to making judgments, controlling impulses and gaining insight into situations. Of course all of the areas of the brain continue to develop and be refined throughout our experience and learning and this is particularly true of the frontal lobes where significant development continues right through to adulthood.[19]

The characteristic plasticity of the developing human brain is thought to be a significant factor in our success as a species.[20] This is because it enables adaptation to the environment in which we find ourselves in our first years of life as the brain continues to develop. The so called **nature-nurture**[21,22] debate has moved on significantly and it is now accepted that it is the interaction between genes and environment which combine to influence our individuality. Certain responses are present from birth, such as being able to mimic and preferring face-like visual representations, but many are learned as the brain develops and interaction with the world around us increases.

Babies are undoubtedly able to engage and make connections with adults even in their earliest days. But it is important to acknowledge that without a reciprocal response from the adults, this so called 'drive' to connect reduces. So during the first period after birth whilst the baby is able to show preferences for familiar rather than unfamiliar, they are also finding out about the environment in which they find themselves and their brains are responding to these early experiences. For example, they are experiencing times of distress in the form of hunger, not something they would have experienced in the womb when nutrition was automatically provided. Baby's brains are responding to the way in which this distress is alleviated.[23] This will include, for example, whether it is for an extended or brief period, whether the amount of food provided is too little or enough and whether it is provided in an emotionally sensitive manner or a harsh uncaring manner. We can see this when babies are more easily soothed by familiar adults who are skilled in reading their signals and cues. For example, holding the baby in a particular way, which we have learned makes sure they feel safe and relaxed, is more likely to reduce their distress. In addition, adults who are tuned into the babies are able to read their signals about the amounts of stimulation that are suitable at particular times.

By being keenly aware of the baby's responses we can recognise that they turn away when over stimulated and are open eyed and alert when engaged, and when they are showing early signs of tiredness and hunger. Having noticed and acknowledged the message the baby is communicating the adult is able to reciprocate and respond appropriately to the baby's current emotional state.

By moderating the levels of stimulation in response to the baby's interest and tiredness, the adult is also helping the baby to experience sensitive emotional regulation. These experiences begin to demonstrate to the child ways of regulating their emotions. Over time, adult support to regulate feelings appropriately will contribute to young children's developing ability to self-regulate their emotional responses.

Building relationships

Cultures vary geographically and over time. For example, child rearing practices will be different in the north of Scotland compared to southern Italy. There will also be differences between parenting practices in each of these locations in the 1800s compared to 21st century. Each culture in each time develops norms which are evident in approaches to parenting.[24]

Early relationships with babies were once thought to be mainly adult directed and initiated. Now of course we are much more aware of the ways in which even newborns strive to make contact and engage others.[25] Even at this early stage it is noticeable that each relationship in which the baby participates is unique and different. The behaviour and response of each player in the relationship affects that of the other.[26] For example, if the baby giggles and laughs when tickled and bounced around by a parent they will respond to these signals by continuing the play. If the baby does not feel safe or at ease when being tickled or bounced they will be more likely to cry or at least look uncomfortable and the parent will respond to these signals by changing the activity. In the immediate situation this difference in response may relate to the baby's tiredness, hunger or fullness, but over time a pattern emerges where they associate particular responses with particular people. This anticipation and familiarity contributes to children's early understanding of how relationships work.[27]

As the baby becomes able to focus on objects more clearly and others share their interest,

a different kind of connection develops. The interaction now has two people engaging each other's attention toward a third item in which they both show interest. This is described as **joint attention** and is a significant change in social engagement. The recognition that someone else is sharing your interest in an object or event is a feeling as well as a cognitive understanding. It is a core, emotionally meaningful experience that underpins the complexities of later understanding about relationships.[28]

A further development that contributes to such understanding is the realisation that once out of sight an object continues to exist. This '**object permanence**' can be seen to impact on young children's early responses to both toys and familiar adults moving out of sight.[29] The child's experience over time will establish their understanding of the likelihood of reappearance. The game 'peek-a-boo' characterises this understanding and can be an enjoyable way for a child to play with this idea.

The experience of familiar and important adults leaving and returning is also integral to Bowlby's concept of **attachment**. The quality of a baby's attachment relationships to parents, carers and close family provide a context for future relationships. Although each relationship will have unique characteristics and vary according to daily experience, by maintaining a warm sensitive nurturing quality they will positively support development. From a secure base of reliable and predictable relationships a child builds a sense of self that enables them to be sufficiently confident to explore and extend their learning beyond their immediate environment.[30]

Fuelling growth and development

To support the rapid growth and development in the womb and during the early years of a child's life, access to an appropriate balance and quantity of food is of course essential. During pregnancy this highlights the need for the mother to ensure her own healthy, nutritious eating and consider the impact on the baby of her food and drink choices. In fact there has recently been a concerted effort by health professionals to highlight concerns about the implications of low birth weight for future development. Parents are often bombarded by advice from a range of sources including extended family, friends, magazines, television and a range of internet sources. Some of these will be very sound and appropriate but others will not. The difficulty is in knowing which is which and being able to access the right ones for your individual situation and child.

It is not just the health and wellbeing of the child which is important though. Looking after children can at times be a difficult and exhausting job and the health of individual parents will impact in a variety of ways.[31] The initial period when the baby is at home can be characterised by little sleep and high levels of anxiety as well as joy, an emotional rollercoaster which in itself is tiring. These often extreme levels of tiredness that come from consecutive nights of interrupted sleep will reduce tolerances, increase frustration and can trigger emotional outbursts in the most placid of us. If eating also becomes spasmodic and less healthy the ability to cope can be further reduced. Most parents will experience at least some days, in these early stages, when it all feels very difficult. It is also a time when extended family, friends and social networks can be of tremendous practical and emotional support. Isolation at this time can heighten anxiety and reduce feelings of competence and confidence. Some mums often comment, for example, on how they miss adult conversation and experience a sense of loss for their individual identity.

Maintaining a generally healthy lifestyle can really help with energy levels and sense of wellbeing. If the wellbeing and health of the

---

Development Matters (available from **www.early-education.org.uk**) supports practitioners, alongside parents and colleagues from other agencies, to identify whether a child is showing typical development, may be at risk of delay or is ahead for their age. When using *Development Matters* it is however important to remember that babies and young children develop at their own rates and in their own ways.

The *NHS Choices* website (**www.nhs. uk**) can help support parents with a range of issues related to pregnancy and the early years of a child's life. The resources are also a good common focus for discussions with the health visitor or midwife.

parents is good this will contribute to the provision of an emotionally supportive and calm environment for the baby.

Real lives, real worries, real struggles

Family life varies considerably and within each family there will be times when things are generally going better than others. Stress levels of the individuals and of the family as a whole will vary according to economics, health and events such as moving house, losing employment, relationship breakdown, bereavement or loss. Each of these events can have a catastrophic effect on a family and may, temporarily at least, make things very difficult. It is also likely to compromise the capacity of parents to be emotionally available and supportive of their child.[32]

During such stressful and difficult times individuals rely on resilience and emotional resources which they have accumulated through previous life experiences. How does that parent who has just been made redundant and is struggling to pay the bills still manage to get up in the morning and bring the children to your setting? The motivation and determination that they muster everyday are significant strengths. Where support is offered it must be in the context of recognising these strengths and adding to them.

Parents who are feeling confident and capable are able to put their child's needs before their own and are emotionally able to nurture

their children. The early relationships that characterise the first few months of a child's life are key to providing a secure foundation for their future feelings of security and emotional wellbeing. A major change that will impact on both children and adults in a family is the arrival of a new baby. For the whole family this event can completely change the dynamics of relationships in a family. For a two year old, who is just beginning to sort out how relationships work this will be much more confusing.[33] The early days are inevitably focused on getting to know the baby as an individual and adjusting to their eating, sleeping and wakeful times. Parents are individually and collectively adjusting to their new family. Even though this may be a second or third child, changes are necessary to accommodate the newcomer.

Time and attention are in great demand as each individual copes with the changes in dynamics. Those who previously were centre stage are now, at least temporarily, relegated to support roles as the baby's demands take precedence. For those who are old enough to understand why, this can be hard enough, but for other children in the family this can be a very confusing and unsettling time.

Two year olds will often use their behaviour as a means of communicating their need for attention, reassurance and support. In such circumstances this can become a tense, irritable and emotionally challenging time for all concerned. If all goes well this potentially turbulent episode in the family's life will pass and things will settle into a new pattern

Reflecting on my practice: thinking about being a parent

Our own experience of being parented will influence what we think about being a parent. This is not to say that we will always do things the same way as our parents, in fact we may consciously do the opposite. As individuals we may have clear ideas about when we want to have children and what it will be like. Our partner will have different ideas resulting from their different life experiences. Somehow we will bring both these perspectives to our roles as parents. Once the baby is born the reality may feel very different from either of our expectations. The way in which we, as two individuals, are able to support each other and together feel the joy and excitement of our new baby creates our family.

As a practitioner, you may also be a parent, and you may work in the same community in which you live or in a very different one. All of these factors will influence your view of the parents you are working with. Maintaining the perspective that the vast majority of parents want the best for their children and wish for them to have a better life than their own, is an important starting point. Looking for and recognising parents' strengths, successes and aspirations, will be the most effective context for conversations that will increase confidence and support for the children.

Two year olds and their characteristic behaviours can be a major surprise to parents and knock their confidence for a while. Watching other parents dealing with a massive meltdown in the supermarket it can be easy to think to yourself that your child will never be like that. However this could only be a certainty if parenting was the only reason and influence on two year olds' behaviour, which of course is not the case. Therefore in reality that meltdown could happen to any of us.

As a practitioner the relationship we have with our two year olds is very different from the relationship they have with their parents. Interestingly, the relationship we have with our own children is also different from the one we have with our two year olds at work. This emotional and contextual difference means that the two year olds will always react differently for us than for their parents and vice versa. It is not simply a case of saying that parents 'just need to do what we do' and all would be easily resolved. However, if we combine some of our professional knowledge and experience with parents' knowledge and understanding, we can gain insights into ways of responding which are most likely to support the two year old through this unsettling time.

including the baby in the life of the family, until another life event comes along to unsettle things again.

For some families, the pressure on individual adults to cope with the emotional demands of putting the children's needs before their own, coping with poor housing or stretching the financial resources far enough, can become a daily battle. Relationships with partners that were thought to be strong and supportive can dissolve under the pressure and reality of the new responsibilities. Illness or health concerns either for the baby or the adults can prolong those early tensions, meaning that daily life becomes unrecognisable as it is dictated by hospital visiting, medical appointments and caring responsibilities.

All these factors mean every child will have a very different initial experience of family life. The state in which they find the adults, and the relationships that develop with siblings, combine to inform their early experience of how the world works.

> *Relate* offers advice, relationship counselling, sex therapy, workshops, mediation, consultations and support face-to-face, by phone and through their website **www.relate.org.uk**

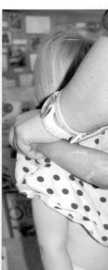

Reflecting on my practice

In relationships between parents and practitioners there are often times when it is more difficult to engage positively. Often this is because one or other of the adults is unsure about how most effectively to respond to a child's behaviour. This scenario depicts a time when the parent is likely to be feeling self conscious, possibly embarrassed and anxious. The practitioner needs to try to find a way to engage the parent in a positive way to lead towards offering appropriate help.

Jessie sees Kylie and her Mum, Janine, walking toward the setting gate. Jessie is Kylie's key person and has known her since she started attending three months ago. Kylie is 25 months old. Kylie is pulling her hand away from her Mum and is beginning to cry. Jessie goes out to meet Janine and Kylie. Janine looks away as Jessie comes near, pulls at Kylie's hand.

Janine: "Stop showing off! I said no sweets!"
Jessie gently puts her hand on Janine's arm and asks if she would like to come to see the photographs taken while Kylie was in the setting the day before. As Janine looks up Jessie claps her hands attracting Kylie's attention,
Jessie: "Shall we show Mummy your castle?"

Kylie looks bemused. Jessie leads them both toward the office to get the photographs. After looking at the photographs and engaging Kylie with a group of children who are playing with some water and guttering outside, Jessie and Janine have a moment for a quick chat.

Janine looks embarrassed and says she must go to work but Jessie just smiles.
Jessie: "Wasn't it great the way Kylie joined the group at the water activity, she really is seeming more confident. What do you think, Janine?"

Janine looks at the clock.
Jessie: "I know we have not got time for a proper chat now but I was wondering if Kylie's new found confidence was also showing in her being more independent about having things her own way at times."

Janine looked puzzled.
Janine: "Her confidence...being independent?"
Jessie: "I wondered if it would be a good idea for us to make a time to talk a bit more about it. I'll think about any examples I have seen here recently. Perhaps you could have a think about times where you think she has been more confident and independent at home and we could talk them through. Together we could then try to give a similar response so that Kylie doesn't get a confusing mix of reactions. Does that sound helpful?"

Janine smiled a little.
Janine: "I don't have to rush home tonight maybe we could try."
Jessie: "Brilliant! It will be really useful to think together about a way to help Kylie with this. See you later, have a good day!"

In what way did Jessie's actions impact on:
■ Her ongoing relationship with Janine?
■ The start of the day for Kylie?
■ Janine's confidence as a parent?
Discuss with colleagues what a helpful script might be for the next conversation between Janine and Jessie.

I am two!

Chapter 2

This is my story

By the time I am two I have a story to tell about lots of things. The highlights of my story give you insights about the understanding I have and the things I can do now. To understand me you need to know about the main characters in my story, where things have happened, what the important events have been and what my everyday experience has been. The story has special meaning for me and must be viewed from my perspective.

Finding out about my culture

Our immediate thoughts when the word 'culture' is mentioned may well be about families and members of our local community who have had different national, ethnic and linguistic experiences than ourselves. However, 'culture' is not just something which belongs to other people.[34] Learning about and questioning our own culture is an important part of understanding how some of the values and views we take for granted have evolved. A simple example would be the way in which most of us consider our age and date of birth to be key information indicating status, life experience, progress and eligibility for certain privileges. Needless to say this has not always been the case and prior to legislation (such as the 1405 Labour Act in England) which deemed that only those over a certain age could work, age was not seen as a significant marker. Our education system is organised by age and so education, age and achievements become linked with expectations. One disadvantage of this can be that skills can be learned out of context rather than being demonstrated and lived via interaction with others in community life. But, for most of us, it is the way it has always been, and few of us would think to question how it has come about.

Our own identity is not just defined by ourselves but by the responses we receive from those around us.[35] For two year olds in our setting, the way in which other children and adults make efforts to connect, show respect and engage with their special people, will inform how they later perceive their individual and cultural identity.

Take this example from Brooker and Woodhead:

"...when Rajae, who is of Moroccan descent, went to fetch her 4-year-old daughter Dounia from kindergarten, the girl jumped into her arms, put her hand on Rajae's mouth and whispered in her ear: 'Please, Mum, never speak Arabic to me again when the other kids can hear you'."[36]

To ensure that our two year olds don't feel like this when they are four, we need to think about the more subtle messages we are giving about our ability to genuinely engage with all parents. One particular danger is when we hear ourselves talking about the 'African way of doing things' or 'a typical same sex couple' or 'the Jamaican culture' as if there is only one way of being in any of these or other groups. The reality is that each family will be developing their own cultural identity that is informed by all of their life experiences, traditions and histories. This engagement has to be more than 'saying the right things'. It has to be deeper and more meaningful. Gathering and understanding parents' reflections on what makes a difference can really help our practice improve as highlighted in this extract from Vandenbroeck's research:

"...the mothers also emphasise that childcare provision offers their children something different from and additional to their home experience: rather than providing a 'home from home', it introduces them to the practices of the wider community. However, each of the mothers explicitly explained how happy she was when the day care centre adopted techniques from her, such as carrying the baby on her back and adapting to the baby's feeding hours or sleep habits. The interviews showed that this careful practice of adapting to the mothers' own habits builds reciprocity in the relationship, and this reciprocity enables mothers to establish hybrid identities for themselves and their children. This in turn empowers the mothers to make their own personal mix of loyalty to their origins and educational habits acquired from the dominant culture without experiencing this as a contradiction."[37]

The difference this quality of relationship with parents will make to our two year olds and their increasing understanding of themselves will be considerable.

 Insights into a two year old's perspective:

I may have been seeing the sofa for two years but now I can walk round it, lift the cushions, climb over it, hide in it, jump off it, smell it, bite it, taste it, throw things at it, push someone else on to it and add all of this to my understanding of 'sofa.' Life is just one big rollercoaster of excitement and learning because I can do so much more than I could. My interests and fascinations are not totally random or indiscriminate though. I am in a way an apprentice.

Being two is a unique time in a child's life. Everything is new because they are seeing and perceiving it with enhanced comprehension and understanding as their thinking, learning and abilities impact on each other. They are gathering skills, abilities and knowledge but also looking to those who know more than them for guidance. Others' actions indicate to them what it is that is important to know about. Their attention is most likely to be captured by what others do rather than what they are saying. The things which many bigger people do and do frequently will be communicated as being important to the two year old. A current obvious example is seeing children picking up a range of objects, holding them to their ear and saying something which sounds like 'hello'. This imitating of the actions involved in using a mobile phone is so common because children are seeing most adults using a phone frequently in many places. This intensity and frequency suggests it must be important for the two year old to know, 'everybody does it everywhere therefore I must need to do it too'. Our moment by moment modeling of how the world works gives all children and especially two year olds significant messages about how the world works.

Although this should make us take stock of what we are showing our two year olds, in our interactions with other children, parents and colleagues, it is also an opportunity to think about ways in which we can make explicit our thinking to help their understanding. From about 10 months, children will typically look to a known adult when a new or unfamilar situation arises. This process of seeking cues from a trusted adult is an important indicator of how the situation is perceived and what would be an appropriate response. Demonstrating and including two year olds in our problem solving and decision making can be particularly useful in building their confidence and skill.[38] Involving children in our conversations as we work out and explore alternative options or solutions, introduces a range of other language but also scaffolds their learning about useful ways to think about challenges encountered.

In this regard the way we engage with children and families, responding to the diversity of their cultures, languages and current life circumstances, will influence our two year olds' developing awareness of engaging with others.

Each of these aspects of life in our setting contributes to our own setting culture and impacts on those who attend, visit or work there. What does our setting culture say to new parents, different groups of parents, individual children and the local community? Perhaps more importantly in what ways can we find out if our intended message is the one that is received.

Thinking about:
what culture means to me

- How would you describe your own family culture ?

- When were you considered to be 'grown up' enough to help with chores around the house?

- What differences were there in the expectations of boys and girls and men and women in responsibilities for household tasks?

- What were the family 'rules' about displaying your emotions when excited, angry, sad, frightened?

- What were the ways in which you were expected to show respect to other members of the family?

- What was a typical family meal time like?

- What is your fondest early memory of your family?

Reflecting on practice:
finding out about family culture

The staff of a day nursery were keen to get to know their current parents a bit better. They organised a picnic in their outdoor area. The staff each brought a dish of their favourite food and asked parents to do the same. As the parents arrived a member of staff met them, accepted their food, and found out how the food had been prepared and why it was a favourite. They took a photograph of the dish of food and made a quick note about why it was a favourite and they did the same for each of their own dishes.

Parents were encouraged to talk to each other about the food they would put on the menu for a family celebration. Menu cards were available so that as parents listened to each other they could make notes of recipes they liked the sound of and whose suggestion it was in case they wanted more details.

Each family and member of staff went away with one new recipe they wanted to try. A display board in the setting was used to put up the pictures, add the children's favourites and pictures of their cooking in the setting. Parents also used the display board to leave messages for each other about the recipe they had tried. Finally, a parent offered to put all the recipes together in a book to sell, which raised money for a trip to the local park following a 'parent cook-in' during which the parents prepared the food for everyone on the trip.

I am two!

Chapter 3
My prime learning

Children's lives in our current society are very different from the lives of their grandparents. One of the most significant changes has been the attitude to keeping children safe. Whilst those of our grandparent's age would have most likely been free to roam the local park and play spaces in the company of their friends with little adult direction, this is now a very rare occurrence.

One result of this shift in thinking is that many children have very little time to explore and revel in the outdoor world. For two year olds in particular the outdoors has major advantages and opportunities. Two year olds, developmentally, are 'all bodies'. That is, they interact and learn from their immediate environment with all of their being. Their physical movements are only just coming under any kind of control, so being outside allows jumping, rolling, pushing and pulling with a sense of freedom unrestricted by knocking over furniture or breaking household items. In this respect being outside is often much safer than being indoors. Two year olds are driven to do things which build their muscles, develop coordination and discover their own capabilities. They will do this wherever they are, so adult attitudes are key to encouraging this type of learning.

The revised EYFS document, implemented in England, from September 2012, builds on the successes of its predecessor. The core principles remain the basis for supporting the continuous improvement of the provision's quality and practitioner understanding of young children's needs. While all areas of learning are important, the 2012 revision of the EYFS recognises that some areas of learning are common to all children regardless of culture and are central to development, whilst others are considered important because they reflect society's current priorities. Therefore the new structure introduced in this revision designates areas of learning as either 'prime' or 'specific' and reflects our increasing understanding of young children's development and learning.

Prime areas of learning

Personal, social and emotional development, communication and language, and physical development are recognised as the three prime areas of learning in the revised EYFS. While all children will be engaged in all areas of learning, these prime areas of learning have particular importance for young children from birth to three years.

The prime areas are described as:

- Time sensitive – whilst they can still be learned later in life they are best and most effectively learned during the earliest years of a child's life

- Universal – wherever children are geographically or historically these areas of learning will be progressing.

Although not dependent on other aspects of learning, the prime areas require caring, nurturing relationships and positive emotional environments to enable development. Crucially, it is important to remember that the prime areas are interconnected and the foundation on which the other areas (referred to as the specific areas of learning in the EYFS) of learning are built.

Personal, social and emotional development

As we have already seen, during the two year old phase there are massive changes in a child's interactions with the world. Development, particularly in these early years, does not occur in a regular step by step pattern. All developmental changes are influenced by the environmental factors previously mentioned, such as health, nutrition and loving nurturing. Each new skill, ability or awareness is initially inconsistent and requires support and encouragement to be consolidated and embedded. At this stage individual systems such as sensory, movement, memory and emotion regulation are developing independent of each other as well as impacting on each other.[39]

Making relationships

A baby's interest in others and recognition of familiar and special people soon develops into a significant social network. Each of these relationships is unique and feels different. As the child matures the differentiation between familiar and unfamiliar is noticeable and trusted adults are relied upon to provide reassurance in new situations.

Taking a social constructivist view, the relationships in which a child engages will provide an important vehicle for their learning. Whether the relationships are with adults or their peer group they will be watching, hearing and learning more about how the world works through attending to how others act and respond.

As children around two begin to explore for themselves ways of joining others in play, and accepting others joining their play, they develop a verbal and behavioural vocabulary to support this process. Although babies and younger children will also make such social entreaties, by two a child's thinking and understanding of themselves and others has developed considerably and involves more complex processes.

Early attempts to make connection with playmates during this phase can often begin with getting physically close. Sometimes too close, standing immediately in front of another child with noses nearly touching can be an initial strategy. In this case there is only a fifty-fifty chance of the next move being shared play or a hand reaching to touch or stroke or hit each other. Effectively scaffolding the process involves providing a dialogue which supports both children's understanding of what is intended. This would include providing the language to ask to play and encouraging giving each other a little more space. For example: 'Julie, do you want to play? Let's make room for us all.'

Looking for the variety of ways in which individual children make contact with playmates is an important basis for building a more comprehensive range of options for different situations. For example, a child whose only strategy is to reach out and swing an arm towards another child to engage them in play, is likely to be frequently misunderstood. By adding a word such as 'play' before, and gradually in place of the physical contact, and ensuring that the child on the receiving end recognises the intent, the play connection can be supported. By watching a group of children it is easy to pick up on the current ways in which they are making contact with each other. Some will get physically close, others will reach out or mirror the play they wish to join. The way of joining play which is least successful, especially in group care situations, is when a child reaches for or takes another's toy. If this is interpreted by the adults around as a hostile act the child whose toy has been taken will understand it in the same way. However, by reframing it as "Aleisha, Josh would really like to play," and then introducing a way in which this could happen, such as adding another tractor or talking about other elements of the farm and how they could be incorporated in the play, a successful outcome becomes much more likely.

With appropriate support and scaffolding there are increasingly successful engagements with other children and the development of shared play begins. A core element of a relationship is the connection in thinking and shared understanding of a situation or event, a meaningful connection mutually understood by the two people involved. This begins in early experiences of joint attention, attachment relationships and parental **'mind mindedness'.**[40] This sense that someone else understands us and is thinking the same thing as us is a basic human experience. The essence of someone 'holding us in mind' and demonstrating that they have been thinking of us even when we are not present is a significant element in experiencing a positive relationship. In addition, our two year olds will be gaining other skills and abilities which contribute to

the development of their social competence, a major part of which will be understanding related to themselves as individuals.

Self-confidence and self-awareness

In particular for a two year old there are important developments happening which relate to the prefrontal cortex part of the brain. This area of the brain takes a long time to fully develop, usually through to adulthood, so at two the process is just beginning. The function of this area is to enable planning, organising, predicting outcomes and self monitoring. The prefrontal cortex does not work alone and is influenced by the processing of information which happens in other areas of the brain. This includes the integration of sensory information, detection of threats and current hormone levels. For example, cortisol, which increases when someone is under stress.[41]

The process of coordinating responses in the brain, including linking emotion, memory and environmental information, controlling the focus of attention, self regulation of behaviour, and prioritising one action or response over another, is often referred to as executive function.[42] As these processes develop individually they also increase their impact on each other, which for a two year old is likely to mean that the way in which they are able to make sense of the world can change dramatically, even over the space of a few weeks.

Our two year olds are developing an awareness of the range of emotions they can experience and learning from those around them ways in which these can be communicated, regulated and sensitively supported. From this awareness builds the ability to name and recognise these feelings in themselves and others. Again this needs those around the two year old to consider carefully how this is done so that it builds on current understanding and makes sense in the real world.

One way in which young children begin to explore their own understanding of emotions, around the age of two, is through pretend games. Being able to pretend involves some complex thinking, including the developmentally significant ability to hold in mind a representation of reality, while being involved in a make believe world. This ability to use symbolic thinking is also important for the development of language.

Although children do engage in solitary pretend play it is also a significant shared activity. Initially, two year olds are best able to take part in pretend play with support and are likely to move in and out of pretence readily. They are beginning to move beyond joint attention into connecting minds with others through creating shared pretence. Being able to sustain the shared pretence takes practice. The development of independent pretend play is usually based on familiar experiences before the later extension to the fantastical worlds of their unlimited fully developed imaginative thinking.

One of the earliest opportunities for children to experience shared thinking with their peers is through pretend play where the meaning is shared and play development is mutually decided. Pretend play has been found universally in all cultures where research

has explored the concept and even in the very few where it is discouraged by adults, children continue to pretend when adults are not present.[43] The emergence of engaging in pretend play is also uniform across cultures, being seen in the majority of children by about 18 months.

The pretend context is a very useful for working out and playing with consequences, emotions, language, sequences of actions and events that we don't really understand. It gives the opportunity to explore without the actual real life consequences. For example, we can stop it when we want and we can rewind and run the sequence of action again differently. In this way, it is an important vehicle for working out how the world works and why people might be responding in particular ways. This insight then contributes to understanding of both self and others and engagement in relationships.

The further development into role play, where a child takes on a particular role and seems to try out what the world looks like through, for example, a superhero's eyes, is the beginning of understanding perspective taking. This type of thinking is important for future moral understanding and empathy.[44] To be able to see a situation or event from the perspective of another person is a skill that is integral to our social understanding and successful relationships. Encouraging and scaffolding our two year old's pretend play is crucial to several aspects of later learning and understanding whether it is superhero play, acting out their fears or rehearsing ways to engage others in play. Most importantly though it is great fun!

Managing feelings and behaviour

The process of understanding emotions, not just happy and sad but starting to understand ourselves through self-reflection, self-awareness and self-regulation, will also impact on these executive functions. This increasing understanding of ourselves enables emotion based identification with others and is linked to beginning to demonstrate understanding of others. As Rogoff explains: "emotion organises all aspects of behaviour and is organised by other aspects of development."[45] In addition, understanding of these aspects of emotion are transformed by the expectations and evaluation of those around us. This complex interlinked process which is beginning to be established for two year olds underpins many of the characteristic behaviours which are associated with this age range. Experiences

are built up gradually to inform this process and the familiar sequence of:

- If I do this what happens?
- If I do this with you what happens?
- If I do this with someone else what happens?
- If I do this today with you what happens?
- If I do this in another space what happens?

This list is endless but the key message for the adults is that at this phase in understanding children are not setting out to do the wrong thing to wind you up. They are trying to work out how the world works and what exactly it is that is causing a particular response. The temptation for an adult is to escalate their response when an undesirable action is repeated.

This is based on a 'I've told you once so you now know it is wrong therefore you have deliberately chosen to do the wrong thing and need a stronger message to stop you doing it' kind of approach. Developmentally this does not really fit with our understanding of a two year old's thinking. A more effective approach is to continue to give a very consistent, calm but firm response. For example, 'stop, put the box down' repeated calmly rather than escalating volume, tone and use of additional words.

Given the drive to explore the world, its contents and every combination of action and interaction that most two year olds have, the responses they get from the adults around them can just be a whole lot of 'No!' While it is of course important to keep our two year olds safe, it is crucial to keep a perspective on their experience. Giving them the message that exploration in general is not a good thing will have longer term implications for their learning and approach to life. Thinking through for ourselves why we might say 'no', whether it is really necessary and what the alternatives might be, can significantly reduce the battles and the frustrations. Engaging with the interests of two year olds can give unexpected insights into what their motivation might be. For example, a two year old playing with the door handle may be trying to get out of the room which adults may need to avoid. However, they may be focusing on the actual working of the handle and have no thoughts of escaping. Only by being alongside the child in this activity can you find out where their thinking is in the moment. One session of pulling the handle up and down, looking at the

bit that goes in and out and the handle on the other side may well satisfy them and prevent an unnecessary battle.

Undoubtedly, there are situations where 'no' is important but if it is used in the context of our understanding of realistic developmental expectations and knowledge of the unique child we are more likely to be supporting their learning than hindering it. There are also interesting themes which children can be working through in their understanding of rules, boundaries and how they relate to them individually. A father of a child who was nearly three, insightfully noted that for a two year old, rules were perceived as random and unpredictable. At three years, they were remembered and should be rigidly enforced for everyone and at four years, they were known but the drive was to find how all these weird exceptions worked.

It is unlikely that a two year old will escape without at some point reacting in a way that could be described as a 'tantrum.' The definitions of the word 'tantrum' are varied and I would encourage thinking of it as being 'overwhelmed by our emotions' as a first step to preparing ourselves to deal with them effectively without damage to ourselves or our two year old. Whether it is frustration at not being able to do something or being told we cannot do something or a range of other triggers, the result is a flood of emotion.[46]

 Insights into a two year old's perspective:

'It is so overwhelming that I am consumed by emotion and not able to access my thinking. The context is that many of my systems which are developing are out of sync. I am able to control my hand and finger movements much more effectively than a couple of weeks ago so I am feeling competent, but I do not yet have the dexterity to thread the string through the loop to hoist the flag on my pirate ship. Immediately I sense my world falling apart, it won't work, I can't do it, the whole world is wrong. I feel the wave of emotion build and overwhelm me. Although, at other times in the day I have been able to use my thinking and learning to do some amazing things, at this point I cannot access any of that thinking.'

Similar things happen to adults, we get very cross when the computer crashes or the car won't start or we are very nervous about an interview. Our minds go blank and we cannot access the thinking which we need to resolve the situation or answer the question. Thankfully, because our brains and its systems have had longer to develop, we are more able to override our emotional response to the extent that we do not throw ourselves on the floor or scream loudly; although at times even for adults it is a close run thing.

So, given that these 'tantrum' situations are likely to happen, what can adults do to help? Such emotional times are scary experiences for the child and the key message that they need from adults is that they are safe, emotionally and physically. This message is most effectively given by talking calmly, acknowledging that the child is feeling cross or sad or upset but that when they are ready we will try to help. Too much language is not helpful at these times but repeated phrases can be helpful, such as 'I can see you are cross', and then, after a pause, 'when you are ready we can try together.' While still emotionally overwhelmed it is not the words which will impact but the calm voice with the understanding that things have been difficult. This approach is most likely to support a growing awareness of being able to regulate emotions while they are still feeling emotionally safe. Telling the child to stop crying or threatening some further action such as going to their room, or going into time out is inappropriate, because when a two year old is this overwhelmed, it is impossible to suddenly change a response.[47]

Communication and language

The development of language is often considered and referred to as an aspect of cognitive learning. However this overlooks the basic reason and process of learning to use language which is the social connection and sharing of culture.[48] A significant point to bear in mind is the wide age range at which verbal language is demonstrated by individual children, with production of ten words being achieved anything from thirteen months to two years and sometimes beyond. As early years practitioners we immediately have an interest in why this might be and what we might do to make a difference.

Listening and attention

The most obvious influence is the quantity and quality of language that babies and toddlers hear around them. This is not just about the words themselves but the tone, intention, motivation and emotion which is communicated with them. The phrase "what are you doing?" can be an indication of fascination and supportive interest or extreme anger depending on how it is said. At this early stage in children's learning about communication they will be more influenced by the tone than the actual words. Further, the words and communication around the child that influences their early motivation to use words will be laden with emotional and social meaning. For example, a child living on a farm will learn the words 'cow' and 'tractor' because they are an important part of their daily experience and are representative of their familiar and immediate world. These words have meaning beyond their role as nouns in the English language. They are significant in the way they are used by those around the child to connect with each other and communicate meaning. Similarly, words are quickly linked together in pairs or phrases to move on from simple naming. For example, a child in town may quickly recognise and use the word 'bus' but extending it even just to 'red bus' adds more meaning to a shared understanding with those around.

This shared meaning is not just a naming of colour and a vehicle but has social meaning that 'I see and travel mainly on red buses'. In areas of the country other than London for example buses are less likely to be red and children less likely to talk about 'red buses'.

Where infant and parents share in joint activities, interpreting each other within familiar contexts, sharing attention to objects in play,

in caretaking, in 'reading' together, or in other kinds of experiences, familiar and novel, such as shopping or visiting the doctor, children learn about language through its use by those around them, in a functional way and in a social context.[49]

A key part of the whole process of learning about communication and language is the developing ability to direct and focus our attention. From the early stage of fleeting attention that is 'caught' by anything interesting, there is a long journey to being able to direct our own attention and focus it on something particular. Sometimes two year olds may appear to be deliberately ignoring an adult who is asking them to do something. However, it is important to remember that from fleeting attention children develop rigid attention to their own activities when even calling their name may not result

in them being able to shift their attention from what they are doing. This rigid attention develops gradually (usually between two, three and four years of age) into single channelled attention where children can shift to a different task, initially with adult support and then on their own. This phase then progresses between three and five years of age into the ability to integrate attention, such as looking down at a book and listening to instructions.

This is a long process and at any stage of this development, paying attention will be particularly difficult if the requirement is to focus on something we have been told to be interested in rather than our own choice.

Understanding

Our two year olds will be particularly interested in language that is useful to them, to name the things which fascinate them, describe important events and to contribute to conversations with their special people. They will play with words and language in contexts where they are useful. For example, outside in their den, they are more likely to explore vocabulary connected to their play when they need the words rather than some unconnected time later when an adult is asking them about it.

Rhyme, rhythm and song using home languages, signing and associated actions should be a joyful part of everyday in your setting. It is one way to engage parents and children in creating a welcoming culture where everyone is able to add their own favourites. Sharing the words and tune in a variety of ways means that families can all extend their repertoire. Most settings now have their own website or computer and could have a recording of a singing session available for parents to use with their children.

Enjoying books and stories should also be a big part of the setting's ethos. Understanding how language works is the basis for later reading and writing. Enjoying good quality books together lays the foundations for understanding how a story formed of words and pictures works on the printed page. Telling stories also helps young children begin to understand how we structure a tale, the importance of the words used and how some phrases are common across many different stories. Settings can encourage parents to use books and stories with their children by sending books as well as story sacks and story boxes home.

Two year olds are working with a range of different levels of comprehension of language in all its different forms at any one time. Following instructions in some contexts will be easy, when the situation and routine are familiar, but much harder if in a new situation or given by an unfamiliar adult. The language around making choices is easy if a child is used to it, but changing the phrase while they are still learning about the process of making a selection, will throw them completely. We therefore need to sensitively understand each child's progress and current confidences to inform our appropriate responses.

Speaking

Gathering, holding and manipulating words is a tiring and complex business when you are new to it, whether in your first, second, third or fourth language. Recognising familiar phrases and words in the sea of language around us is a huge relief as we try to make sense of it all. Our two year olds are full of energy and absorbing enormous amounts of information and new learning throughout the day. Times of relaxation in a place that soothes and helps them feel at ease is essential to their healthy progress. Being sensitive and alert to when and where our two year olds are most relaxed and ideally able to sleep is a vital task as a key person. Extending the possibilities so that children can show their preferences can be a significant factor in meeting individual children's needs. Listening to parents' information about sleep routines, relaxing times and signals that children are tired, are necessary conversations to build a shared

understanding of children as individuals.

The joy of being with a two year old is the opportunity to see the world with fresh eyes. There is such a sense of wonder and excitement in their eyes and faces. In fact it radiates from their whole bodies as they see something of interest. Their exploration and engagement gives us the opportunity to offer a range of language which names, describes links to other experiences, interests and most of all communicates that we are interested too and that we are sharing in the experience with them. Most importantly though our interactions with our two year olds should be encouraging them to talk with us, have conversations about their interests. The way in which we demonstrate taking part in a conversation, listening, looking, linking what we say to a previous contribution, responding to the emotional as well as verbal messages will be a significant model to scaffold their understanding of both language and the process of communicating.

The process of building language and communication skills is a long and difficult one with complex learning about words, their meaning and the different ways in which they are used. It is also a process that is loaded with emotion and messages about self-worth, competence and skill levels. Each and every interaction makes a difference to how children feel about themselves and the way they perceive how others view them. Engaging all adults in recognising this reality and working together to make this a positive experience will contribute to a secure foundation for future relationships and learning.

Physical development

Some adults still feel very protective about two year olds and are sometimes more anxious now that the 'baby' is on the move. It can be tempting at times to think about the buggy, highchair or car seat as a place to keep them 'safe'. Getting the right balance for two year olds' freedom of movement and time inside and outside is increasingly being recognised as essential for healthy all round development.

Moving and handling

Through the experience of being two, children can discover the joy of independent movement in all sorts of ways. Initially our two year olds will be very focused on the mechanics of coordinating their movements and therefore not able to also think about any possible danger. Going up and down stairs takes some working out and two year olds will usually have a range of strategies including bottom shuffling, coming down backwards or holding a hand. It is important that they have these opportunities to problem solve and explore different ways of doing it but adult supervision is of course essential. They will also get stuck at certain obstacles. For example they may have found a successful way of going up and down stairs but stop suddenly at the doorstep.

Learning about ourselves physically is not just about being on the move all the time. We must provide an appropriate environment to allow children to find comfortable body positions, which support their attention focus rather than giving energy and focus to 'sitting still' in a way that the adult thinks is best for them. Equally, sitting at a table is seldom appropriate for two year olds, except to join family or group mealtimes. Even then, there will be times when a picnic style arrangement will be more appropriate. Finding out about being comfortable and at ease with how the body of a two year old moves and the way in which we, as practioners, organise them is interconnected with our view of ourselves as individuals and our self-awareness.[50]

In the same way that developments in the brain have an impact on our social understanding and vice versa, the same is true as connections are established between areas of the brain and the muscles in our bodies. Through actions being repeated and modified the brain is able to predict more accurately the combination of movements which are required in order to complete a desired task. The process for two year olds is about building up experience of doing something in a range of ways and situations so that the brain can have a secure base for predicting the outcomes of a range of motor movements. This then leads to the ability to be able to refine control and develop mastery over the complexity of an action. For example, discovering the difference between gently holding someone's hand and gripping it really tightly takes a lot of practice. The brain needs a range of information to facilitate the appropriate amount of pressure required to hold hands with a friend. This will include making adjustments for big hands and little hands, doing the action quickly or slowly, intertwining fingers or having a palm to palm wrap, keeping contact when both are moving and so on. All in all a complex set of movements which the brain can only successfully master once a wide range of sensory information is gathered and processed to inform future attempts at hand holding. The same of course is true of the full range of movements from gross motor coordination to intricate and delicate precision manipulation.

 Insights into a two year old's perspective:

There are a range of ways in which we use sensory feedback to understand the world around us. Feeling the pressure of our bodies against another surface whether the floor, a wall or another person, gives us sensory feedback about where we begin and end. Rough and tumble play engages our bodies and senses in working out where different bits of us are in space, in relation to others and the rest of our bodies. A cuddle or a hug with a special person can give me that restful reassurance that all my body is enveloped and I can feel all the tension in my body relax. Games of rolling in a blanket can be another way of children enjoying this sense of ease. Recognising over time what my body does and how it feels also enables me to explore changing the amount of pressure and strength I use in holding things, leaning against things, rolling on things.[51]

Our experience of feeling the wind, rain and snow changes in weather. Being connected with the natural things around us is integral to our learning about ourselves and what affects our wellbeing. For example, recognising that we feel different in wide open space than in small enclosed spaces and whether these are inside or out. These physical differences will affect our emotional state, inform our ability to regulate our bodies and influence our wellbeing.

Health and self-care

It is not just our physical skills that develop when we do physical things. If a two year old engages with others with a purpose and shared intent they will be mirroring the movements of others, adding to their strength as they push, pull, and lift. Throughout they will be making decisions and problem solving.

Their increasing interest in being independent can be helped by creating situations where they can learn about making choices.

For example:

- choosing between two options of what to wear
- deciding if they need a coat and wellies
- selecting things they need to put in the bag to take with them
- taking their scooter or a ball to the park.

Just saying out loud the thinking that we go through before making such decisions can support our two year olds to make informed decisions. This pattern of decision making can also support mealtimes. This does require some prior thinking by the adults about suitable food and situations where the two year old has a 90% chance of being successful.

While in the setting we can adapt our routines for most mealtimes, for parents this may not be so easy. In normal circumstances, rather than putting food on the plate, try letting children serve themselves from a larger dish on the table. This gives them a chance to try out different sizes of portion and perhaps come back for more. When introducing this way of organising mealtimes, it is also a good idea to offer food that is liked and easy to eat. As well as offering the opportunity to practice decision making about how much they take, it is a context for using the physical coordination skills of getting the food on the plate.

Another big transformation in the lives of two year olds is the whole toileting process. While having nappies changed, two year olds are able to co-operate by moving their legs and lifting their tummies to accommodate the process.

Of course, this is most likely to happen when the adult takes time to engage in a sensitive and 'tuned in' sort of way so that it becomes a shared activity. Singing songs, tickling games, conversations and telling stories will all help to make this a happy experience for children and adults. Wherever possible giving children a choice of who changes their nappy can help them to feel at ease and give them increasing control over the situation.

Gradually they will have an growing awareness of other children using the toilet and be curious about why. This and the gradual recognition of when they need to urinate or defecate will lead, with some encouragement, to using the potty or toilet. The level of physical activity and range of ways of moving a child explores will have a direct impact on the muscle tone around internal organs and particularly the bowels. This is likely to influence when they recognise the sensations related to needing to go to the toilet and having control over the process.

Tuned in adults can really help by looking for early signals that children are needing to go to the toilet. This might include changes in concentration levels, perhaps running around and maybe being still or unable to be still - it will be different for each child. Reflecting back to the children sensitively that you have noticed the change and wonder if they might need to go to the toilet, leaves the decision with them but focuses their attention on a possible early warning signal.

I am two!

Chapter 4
Starting the journey

First contact

Starting the relationship with parents can feel daunting to both sides of the relationship. That uncertain feeling about how others will react to us, appraise or judge us seems to be ever present in the human condition. Practitioners are often heard to say how good their relationships with parents are but equally, when asked which area of work engenders most concern, relationships with parents features very highly. Although there are many similarities between different cohorts of parents there are also many differences. We are all individuals and in the same way that changes in staffing will impact on the relationships with parents, each individual parent will impact on the dynamics of the parents as a whole group.

As a practitioner you have more experience of your setting based on the fact that you spend more time there over a day, week and year. You are therefore more familiar with the physical layout, the way things are done, the tone of the staff relationships, the level of organisation and support and the quality of the provision for the children. Your overall view is built up over time and influenced by your experiences of being in or hearing about other settings. This familiarity can lead to you paying less attention to the detail of the environment, making assumptions about the information and messages that are given. Ultimately it can lead to a level of complacency which endangers the quality of the provision as a whole.

Only by consciously finding different ways to gain a fresh view of your own setting can you sustain and improve the quality. What was effective with the staff, parents and children of last year will not necessarily work for those with you this year. Even those who continue to be with you from last year will have altered perspectives because of their ongoing experiences.

The first contact a parent has with your setting, whether by phone or face to face, is an important first impression. The degree to which you are able to demonstrate genuine engagement, interest and a positive intent will impact on all future interactions with each parent and also on parents as a group. Making stereotypical comments about the 'terrible twos' can shut down conversations and convey that we think two year olds are terrible and need to be controlled. In contrast, listening to and understanding parents' aspirations and expectations of their children can begin a supportive and rewarding journey for both parties.

Building everyone's confidence

As a practitioner your professional development includes building confidence in engaging appropriately with each and every parent. Some days are more trying than others, some of us feel shy, some situations are more anxiety making than others. Ultimately, it is learning about interacting with individual people, some of whom for many reasons we may not choose to spend time with socially but with whom we are professionally required to welcome, engage and support appropriately. The most important reason being that by doing so we are most able to help and support the children's wellbeing and development. This needs to be a recurrent focus in appraisal or performance management, as well as supervision because it is something we can always improve and learn more about.

It is not just staff confidence that is an issue. Most parents, at one time or another, experience anxiety or lack confidence in their role as parents. A recent Scottish government report[52] collated the views of 1500 parents. While there were many positive aspects of parenting, the report also noted situations where parents would like more support, including 'how to confidently support children's range of emotions including advice and tips about handling temper tantrums'.

Each child responds differently to family circumstances and attending early years provision. Also each change in a child's development presents different challenges for parents. Practitioners are a key source of help and support for parents and can become trusted guides in the confusing world of parenting.

Using secure, up-to-date knowledge of child development alongside direct experience of many children as a basis, parent's observations and concerns can be put into context and a shared understanding of the child as a unique individual built up over time. *Development Matters* provides a useful guide to the progress of typical development and ways in which adults can support the child's learning and development.

An effective strategy for building confidence in engaging with parents is to reflect on successful interactions which have enabled parents to talk about concerns, share ideas about ways forward and agree on immediate actions for home and setting to support the child. The ways in which you have been able to make this happen on one occasion will not be directly transferrable to another, but will deepen your insight into the skills you used and how these might be increased.

Sharing expectations and aspirations

Parents often remark to me that two of the most challenging times with their children are around two years old and again when they are teenagers. Interestingly, similar things are going on at these times with regard to brain development and social, emotional awareness. Two year olds are developing a more comprehensive awareness of themselves as individuals and exploring ways to gain independence, including demonstrating their ability to accomplish things on their own. Their understanding of what it is to be an independent person has come from their observation and experience of those adults and older children around them. No one single observation or experience has led them to respond in a particular way. Patterns of responses communicate the message that this is 'how we respond to each other around here.' As two year olds try to make sense of how relationships and interactions work in daily life they can often seem to lurch from confident, independent individuals to confused, emotionally fragile and frustrated bundles of negative energy. For parents these experiences of dealing with their child who is overwhelmed by their emotions can feel equally overwhelming for them as adults. In similar ways to their child they can experience feelings of incompetence, anxiety, insecurity and major frustration. All of which can be very much what practitioners feel as they navigate the minefield that is supporting children during this developmental process, no matter what chronological age they are.

Under such emotional pressure, often in addition to other family and life stresses, parents can feel particularly isolated during this phase in their parenting. Your own child's behaviour can often feel more extreme, frequent or intense than that of any other child you have known or seen. The opportunity to share concerns, anxieties and worries with a confident professional on a daily basis who has a shared knowledge of your child can be a real life saver. Seeing these typical two year old responses in the context of child development and being reassured about appropriate adult responses and that it really is something most children go through can be a major confidence boost. Recognising that this emotional process is evidence of developmental progress can easily get overlooked. But for an individual human being, beginning to learn that you are a unique autonomous individual is a crucial step, even though its fulfillment is a life long learning process.

Thinking about: genuine engagement with parents

- Which parents have lived longest in the local area?

- Which parents have only recently moved to the area?

- Which of your local Children's Centres do parents use most?

- What are the local sources of information which parents use e.g. library, doctors' surgeries, Family Information Service, local charity or voluntary organisations?

- What kind of information have they found useful?

- In what ways could you facilitate sharing of this information between parents?

- What are parents currently interested in about their children's development?

- Who in the local community could you ask to come and talk with them about this topic?

- Which of the activities currently on offer at your local Children's Centres have you recommended to specific parents?

Reflecting on my practice: using local facilities

While talking with parents whose children were new to her group, Alison realised that several parents were very wary of taking their children to the local park. In conversation she found out that they were worried that their two year olds might hit out at other children when they were trying to join in with play. Their main concern was that the parents of the other child would be cross with them and their child.

Alison wondered how best to build the parents' confidence and increase the chances of the children being taken to the park more often. She downloaded a map of the local area that showed three parks within reasonable walking distance of the setting and put it on the display board near the entrance to the room. She added the question 'Which park do you like best?' and asked parents to add a post it note to vote for the one they liked.

Alison also started talking to each parent about the specific ways their individual two year olds were currently indicating that they wanted to join others play. Some children were tapping another child on the arm, some said 'play', some snatched a toy, some took a toy to a child and some played alongside until they were noticed.

With each parent, Alison discussed how they would like their child to join in with play given their current level of language. This helped Alison and the parent to devise a 'next step' for each child.

A few weeks later, she organised that the staff would take the children to one of the parks for the last part of the afternoon session for three days of the week. The parents were invited to join the outing or collect their two year olds from the park at the end of the day.

Parents began talking with each other and shared the progress their children were making in joining in with play. Several parents arranged to meet each other at the park over the weekend, while others decided to go as a group to one of the other parks nearby.

Chapter 5

This two year old is different from any other you have ever known

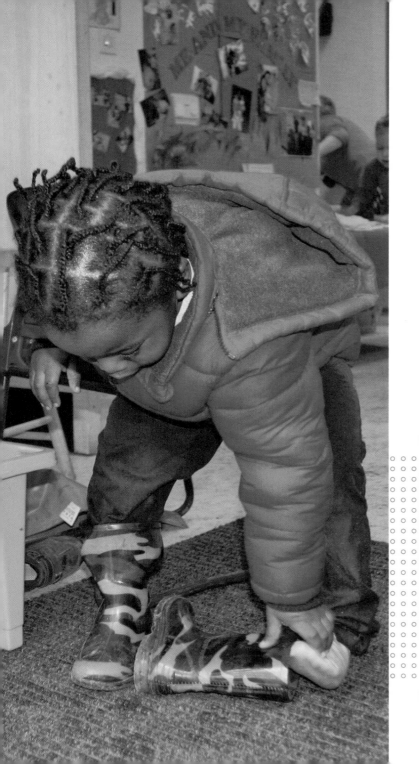

Hearing my story

Seldom are parents reluctant to talk about their children, given the right encouragement. Much important information can be gleaned in those early conversations during first meetings and the settling phase. At worst this process is a form filling exercise. At best any required forms are just there as a catalyst to open up conversation and share knowledge.

During the first five years of a child's life parents are generally in the habit of using the 'My Personal Child Health Record' commonly known as the 'Red Book' (or in some areas the 'Yellow Book') to record together with health professionals the reviews, immunisations, weight, height and personal details relating to the child. This book[53] has several pages towards the end that encourage the parents to record early developmental milestones as well as contact with other professionals. There is also a wealth of information about other appropriate sources of support as well as details of forthcoming health reviews.

In some areas practitioners use these booklets to talk with parents in preparation for their next health visitor appointment. It is a greatly untapped resource that can be used as a focus for discussion between parents and practitioners. Although completed by the parent, practitioner and parent observations can be included to give the health visitor a much fuller picture of the child's progress over time. The early details can prompt useful discussions between parents and practitioners about the child's birth, early relationships, feeding and general health.

If sharing the 'Red Book' is seen as a regular part of effective practice in sharing information with parents, the EYFS progress check at age two can also be a useful tool to share information between health and early years provision so that there is continuity in the child's story to date. Bringing together the early years practitioner and parent view of the child, offers the health professional additional background to inform their own assessments. Further detail available in Development Matters can inform useful and in depth discussions between parents and practitioners.

In time, it is planned that the health and early years reviews at around two years will become one integrated assessment. There is no reason though why we cannot make the most of existing resources to liaise with health visiting teams locally. This will help to coordinate the gathering of information about two year olds and, with parents, consider different perspectives on each child's progress.

How am I learning when I am with you?

The revised EYFS highlights the 'how children learn' as well as the 'what they learn'. This has been given greater prominence in the revised EYFS by bringing the information together as the 'Characteristics of Effective Learning.'

The three characteristics are described as:

- Playing and exploring
- Active learning
- Creating and thinking critically

Talking with practitioners it is clear that bringing these characteristics together in this way has provided a way of thinking and talking about the real essence of individual children and their approaches to learning generally. As such they also provide a really useful way to begin and develop conversations with parents. Considering the characteristics of effective learning in relation to an individual child, is about describing accurately what we have observed about the way in which they interact with and learn from their environment. These are important insights that inform how we can support children's learning effectively across all areas. Our thinking about children's approaches to learning is informed by these characteristics regardless of the child's age, competencies, development or personality.

I am also struck by the influence that consideration of the characteristics of effective learning have on adults as they think about their own learning.

Questions for practitioners to consider are:

- In what ways do you play with and explore your new learning, engaging more deeply in improving your own practice or relationships?

- What are your current motivations and are they based on values and principles that as an individual you feel are important in all aspects of your life?

- In which aspects of your life do you recognise your creative abilities and critical thinking?

The characteristics as set out in the EYFS have no doubt been compiled with young children in mind. But as the adults who are supporting children in developing their approach to learning, surely it is also important for parents and practitioners to be able to look for and celebrate their own successful approaches to learning. Sadly many practitioners and parents have negative and debilitating feelings about their youthful learning which can become barriers to their own later learning. Being with two year olds is a real opportunity to rediscover the excitement, intensity and fascination of finding out new and different things about people, places, things and our interactions with them.

Two year olds are usually extremely busy learning about everything around them. They are in many ways the embodiment of these characteristics. The unique picture of an individual child's approaches to learning is likely to be recognisable across the two different contexts of home and setting. Therefore both parents and practitioners are able to contribute observations which indicate each of the characteristics.[54]

Throughout the detail of these characteristics as described in *Development Matters*, the importance of access to stimulating opportunities through an enabling environment and the interaction of sensitive adults, is underlined as scaffolding children's thinking and participation. At two, children are closely observing adults' responses to their own actions and will mirror what they observe. Therefore constant comments of 'be careful that's too high/fast' or 'don't that's only for

the big children' accompanied by the worried look and restraining hand on the arm will give a strong message that it is not good to 'have a go', seek challenge or take risks. This kind of playing and exploring is about engaging with the environment and the people in it and whilst adults do need to keep children safe, part of this learning is about children recognising how to make safe decisions about what is too high or fast.

A more useful 'scaffolding' script might include phrases such as: 'where can you hold on? does it feel wobbly? will you move a foot or a hand next?' Also supporting children's risk taking through offering choices can be helpful, such as during a game of 'roly poly' with a blanket where offering 'more' or 'stop now' enables the child to test their own limits as they feel appropriate on any particular occasion, rather than adults assuming that because it was fun yesterday it will be just as much fun today. These are also important opportunities to give children appropriate control over what is happening to them and to demonstrate respectful relationships.

As a practitioner these are interactions and perspectives that you are working with many times a day and discussing with colleagues. As such your understanding and thinking has the opportunity to develop over time and to become honed and more accurate through reflection. Even after a short break it is noticeable that your 'script' with children is not quite as fluent as it was before you left. This interactive script is fluent when you are able to amend it to suit both different situations and to do so subtly when supporting different

children involved in the same activity.

Parents do not always have the benefits of working with other adults to reflect and consider the impact their responses are having. Therefore it is helpful to share real examples and a range of possible ways to support children's engagement and thinking about their activities. Wherever possible empowering parents to take part in setting activities with their children and to talk through the ways in which it is possible to extend and engage children's thinking can be invaluable. More often than not parents have examples from home which, though using different terminology to practitioners, will provide real insight into their children's perspective on their explorations.

relationships with each parent will be different and their unique life experience to date will inform what they think is happening, as well as their role in the unfolding story. In the eyes of a two year old the arrival of a new baby can be traumatic. Firstly, because it changes everything about their daily experience just because it means there is another human being present. If you then take on board that this new human being will need time and attention from the available adults, then the impact on the two year old can be enormous. In reality there is often a period where the two year old struggles to find this new relationship with parents and experiences the sense of loss of the old familiar one.

At two years old understanding of ourselves and others is just emerging, so making sense of such major changes takes time and needs sensitive understanding. Being able to demonstrate the ability to empathise and take the perspective of the two year old in such a situation can be difficult. It takes a lot of skill, flexibility of thinking as well as empathy. Receiving this depth of understanding from a significant adult will be a valuable and meaningful experience for our two year old.

Similarly, the relationships each child has with each member of the team in the setting will be different. This seems obvious but adults often seem puzzled about why children will behave in one way with one member of staff but differently with another. If someone who has shown themselves to be sensitive, supportive and helpful to you, asks you to do something, you are much more likely to comply than if asked by someone who seems

My special relationships

For those who have worked with the EYFS the principle of the 'unique child' is very familiar. However, it is worth taking time to reflect on the fact that each unique child also has characteristically unique relationships with those around them. At home, although all the children in the family may have relationships with the same parents, each of these connections will be different as will those between siblings. Particular life events will temporarily or permanently alter these relationships. The timing of such events will significantly change the impact on individuals. For example, a five year old will understand a parental separation in a different way to a twelve year old. As individuals, their to be constantly telling you not to do things. At times when a child, particularly a two year old, is finding it difficult to manage their response, the sensitive adult is more likely to be able to appreciate what the problem is and find an effective way to offer support. This is not about 'giving in' but it is about having realistic expectations about what children can manage during specific developmental stages and in particular situations. At such times, sharing your thinking and problem solving with parents, can enable both of you to develop your knowledge and understanding of the two year old's perspective and identify effective strategies to manage the situation.

Thinking about: my learning

- What are the surprises, delights and concerns which you have recorded about the two year olds in your key group this week?

- Which delights were the parents able to add when you talked to them about your observations?

- In what ways have you been able to share your observations with the dads of the two year olds in your group?

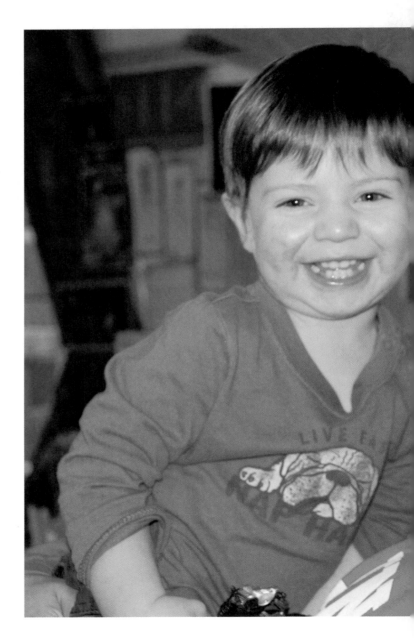

Reflecting on my practice

Caleb's key person, Jamila, noticed he was very tired. Jamila asked his Mum, Hortence, if everything was OK and if he had been sleeping well. Hortence said he hadn't slept well for the past couple of nights and had not seemed tired at bedtime.

Jamila talked with Hortence about whether they should make a change to his nap time in the setting. They decided to see whether there was anything different about his activity level during the day, then talk again.

The next day Jamila explained to Hortence that she had noticed that Caleb was not spending as much time running around outside in the fresh air. She had also noticed that Caleb no longer endlessly played with the water outside, but was getting really interested in story books. Jamila explained to Hortence that they could look at how they could engage Caleb's interest in books with more physical activity.

Between them they chose some books, including 'We're going on a Bear Hunt' by Michael Rosen. Jamila explained that she would look to make some changes to the outdoor area and develop a game based around the story to see whether this would re-engage Caleb in outdoor activity.

Jamila found that by adding a simple 'stage' area with some books, several of the children spent more time there acting out stories and extending their play to other areas of the playground.

By the end of the week Hortence said Caleb was back to being tired at bedtime and seemed to be sleeping much better again.

I am two!

Children's
Profile books

Chapter 6
Keeping the conversation going

Keeping up with my news

Although contact with families is usually daily, and often twice daily, it can be hard for both parents and practitioners to have time available for extended conversations. Building on and maintaining the positive relationship with parents which has been established through the admission process takes effort and some creative thinking.

During the early years children's progress is rapid, variable and inconsistent especially around two to three years,[55] so there needs to be lots of talking to keep a strong connection with the parents. If care is not taken the daily conversations become disjointed. There is also a risk that any difficult topics may be avoided due to a shortage of time. Undoubtedly time is short and the daily contact with parents tends to be early morning and at the end of a long, hard and exhausting day for everyone.

However it is possible with a little conscious thought to bring some coherence to these daily conversations. The benefits are that the relationships have some continuity and are supported rather than being neglected and left to flounder. Importantly, confidence can grow in each other as well as in the relationship. This can mean that if some more difficult topics need to be discussed they take place in the context of a familiar interaction and a positive relationship.

One useful way to begin to increase the coherence of the daily conversations is to think about themes that are common, such as sharing with parents the ways in which

their children are currently indicating to others that they want to play. At two this can range from standing close, taking a toy, running after another child and tapping, to using a couple of appropriate words. The purpose of using such a theme over the course of a week or fortnight is that both adults are looking with interest at a particular aspect of the child's play. They are then both able to make valuable contributions to the discussion.

Using the same theme across a group can be useful to highlight similarities and differences between children in the group for practitioners and therefore inform planning. For parents, recognising the importance of a particular response or behaviour demonstrated by their child, can increase the likelihood of them noticing and being able to build on the practitioner knowledge of the child's experiences outside of the setting through their sharing of their own observations.

Two year olds are trying out many new ways of interacting with their environment as well as with other people. By building a shared view with parents about the patterns of behaviour and response that are emerging in their motivation and engagement, useful adult engagement and strategies can be devised together to support the child's learning.

These short interactions contribute to a clearer understanding of the two year old's life as a whole, not just in the setting. This enables some exploration of what the two year old's experience may be like over a week or month perhaps. For example, what is the balance of time spent outdoors compared to indoors and how much time is spent in 'organised' activities compared to self initiated exploration. The balance wheel at the end of this book may be helpful to support these discussions. Adults are often surprised when they have the chance to consider the two year old's view of life over a period of time.

The omnibus edition

Fortnightly, monthly and termly contact can broaden the areas discussed in the themed daily contact. If current daily themes are focusing on personal, social and emotional development, the fortnightly or monthly discussions might also include communication and language or physical development. Where daily contact with parents does not happen, other forms of communication need to be explored with parents to ensure that communication links support the ongoing relationship. Most parents, given the opportunity, will try to find a practical way to share information and keep in contact whether by phone, email, text or written notes.

From engaging parents in early discussions about why contact is important and negotiating the method and frequency of communication, it is a small step to agreeing themes which would be of particular interest at different stages in children's development. With two year olds for example, parents may be anxious about levels of frustration and how these are dealt with. Taking time to explain the strategies and sharing frequency of incidents between home and setting is not a competition to see who has more or less, but to explore the ways in which adults can enable the child to feel safe and gradually learn to develop useful thinking and ways to alleviate feelings of frustration. For example, for adults to talk through their thinking in potentially frustrating situations can let children see alternative ways to deal with such tricky times. Scripts such as 'I'm sure these bricks will all fit in this box but I can't see how, I wonder who could help me?' seem so simple, but unless children hear us use them and see that they are effective in problem solving they won't be motivated to try them.

Checking how things are going for our two year olds

The revised EYFS now includes the requirement to report to parents on progress their child is making in the three prime areas of learning at around two years old. Details are included in the National Children's Bureau booklet *A Know How Guide*. In the context of the regular contact with parents described above, this is a natural part of your ongoing creation of a shared view of the child's talents and abilities.

However, for a variety of reasons contact with parents cannot always be quite so consistent. It is undoubtedly the professional responsibility of each and every practitioner to make every effort to forge links with and maintain a positive relationship with parents. The two year check offers an opportunity to ensure that the child's needs are being met and development is progressing as expected. However, if this check stands in isolation and not part of ongoing conversation and regular sharing of observations, then the purpose becomes diluted. Health professionals advise that if difficulties or concerns about developmental progress are raised around two years old, the effectiveness of any appropriate intervention is greatly increased, than if left till the child is older.[56] It is also reassuring for parents to understand that while each child develops at their own rate, their child is within the expected ranges of typical development.

In addition to the progress check carried out in the early years setting a health review takes place between two and two and a half years old. Details are available in the 'Red Book'. As previously mentioned, it is intended that around 2014 these two progress reviews will be integrated into one process.

The way in which these two progress checks work locally varies considerably and to make it a coherent experience for families and of maximum benefit for our two year olds, it would make sense for them to be coordinated. This need not be a complicated process. A phone call to your local Health Visiting team will clarify how the reviews are organised in each area.

By highlighting your desire to make sure parents and families have an informed and coordinated set of information about their two year olds, you can explore ways to arrange the timing of the setting reporting to happen before the appointment with the Health Visitor. This provides additional information for the Health Visitor and helps parents to gather their thoughts and questions so that any concerns can be prioritised during the discussion. Children's centres may also have a role co-ordinating these different checks in the local area.

Chapter 7
Noticing

I am two!

This diagram highlights some of the
opportunities to support the family and
break the cycle of poor outcomes

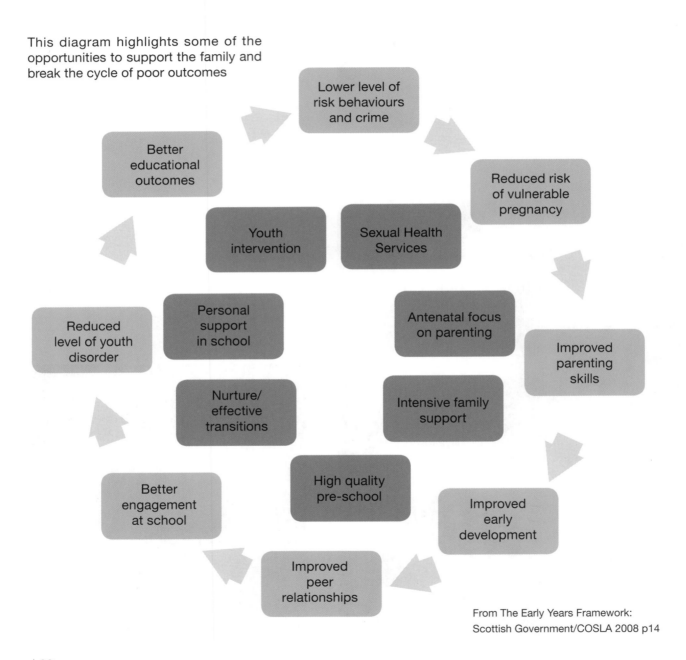

From The Early Years Framework:
Scottish Government/COSLA 2008 p14

The early years of a child's life have been increasingly recognised as both a time of rapid development but also of major vulnerability. Politically, the realisation that this vulnerability has long term consequences is being understood across the party divides. Finding effective ways to improve the chances of every child to have a secure foundation in life remains a major challenge in terms of both policy and consistency of high quality provision. The diagram depicted left shows the significant role which high quality early years provision can play in improving children's life chances.

Sometimes it can be difficult to relate these wider societal and political aims with our day to day practice. However, by focusing our efforts on recognising and meeting the needs of our individual children and their families, we will be able to strive to make every interaction count as a step towards supporting their parents to give them a positive start in life.

Observing and watching carefully

In early years we talk a lot about the importance of observations and using them as a basis for our planning of next steps and opportunities for children's learning. As parents we watch our children a lot of the time and think about what they are doing, often worrying if they are progressing as they should and if we are giving them the best help and support. The two adult activities are very similar, but the more formal version of 'observations' which practitioners talk about can suggest that it is more important, valuable and technically clever.

If we are not careful this can quickly build a barrier in our conversations with parents.

The key processes in gathering information and insights about children's individual development are firstly describing what we see and secondly trying to understand what we have seen. As practitioners, we use *Development Matters* as a guide to typical development, along with our experience of the unique child and children generally to inform our understanding. Parents have specialist knowledge about their children based on seeing them over time, across developmental changes and in a range of contexts which is key to building a shared understanding of the child as an individual. Even a child who is in a setting full time will still be spending 70% of their week elsewhere, most often with parents and family.

We are more likely to be able to understand what we see children doing if we can reflect with parents on the children's reactions in different situations. As adults we respond differently when we are at work than when we are at home or out socialising and the same is true for children. Our shared understanding with parents allows us to gain insights about how the child shows us that they are relaxed, involved, excited, anxious, or frustrated. Being two is a bit of a rollercoaster for children, going from being engaged and intensely involved to overwhelmed by their emotions in a matter of seconds.[57]

Equally, it is often a similar feeling for the adults around them. The signals and insights we gain alongside parents help us to make sense of what is happening for individual children and which of our possible responses is most likely to be useful for them.

Tuning in

There is something almost magical about the feeling of being 'in tune' or 'on the same wavelength' as another person. As adults we seek relationships where this is a reciprocal experience and a sense of belonging, being respected and valued follows with little effort it seems. However, without attention, communication and continued effort, the relationship can lose this special feeling. Each person in the relationship is constantly changing and developing their thinking, following new interests and ideas. If those involved are able to share interest and enthusiasm for these developments the relationship can deepen and strengthen.

For children who are beginning to make sense of a very complicated world of relationships and experiences, the joy of having someone in tune and emotionally alongside you, is both tangible in the moment and memorable over time. The subtleties of how this happens are difficult to accurately describe in words, but let's try. The similarity with early cuddles with a baby, when it feels as if there is no one else there but the two of you is significant. These early attachment relationship experiences underpin later understanding and expectations of how we relate to others.

 Insights into a two year old's perspective:

As a two year old whatever my experience of relationships to date I can delight in the sense that some one is 'on my side', focusing on my fascinations and recognising the changes in my emotions. When I am two my world seems to crash down around me if the final brick I place at the top of the tower brings it tumbling to the floor. In my cries and emotional 'overwhelmedness', the adult who is in tune with me will see my devastation that I can't yet physically place the brick with the accuracy which keeps the tower standing. They also see the frustration that I am trying to understand why bricks do that falling thing when I want them to do a standing up thing. The adult who does not yet understand me and my two year old world will be more likely to see an irritating child making too much noise with bricks, or someone who can't do proper building activities yet.

The response of the two different adults to what they have seen will be dramatic for me and will add to my understanding of how relationships work. In particular, these two different responses will tell me more about how I am viewed by others. The response based on the superficial perspective of me as an irritating and noisy child who cannot do things will contribute to a picture of myself which suggests that I am not valued or competent and that those around me will provide help. I am left to struggle with even more difficult and negative emotions.[58]

With the sensitive and 'tuned in' response I will begin to understand myself as someone who is valued, whose efforts and activities are important. I will also understand that help and support is available from people around me. This combination is more likely to help me try again, persevere and be motivated to explore other ways to make my tower work the way I want it to.

Characteristics

For our two year olds we will be exploring how they are currently learning then find responses which encourage further engagement, celebrate motivation and make visible their thinking. In addition these characteristics give us clear indications about how appropriate our enabling environment and interactions are for our two year olds. If we focus our learning with

parents, on how children learn, together we can find examples where we have been able to understand a little more fully what the child is experiencing.

Thinking about:
Observing and learning

- In what ways do you engage parents to develop a shared understanding of your recent observations?

- How many of your displays around the nursery are based on parent/practitioner observations of the children?

- Do your displays highlight the important learning about behaviour and social understanding which is taking place?

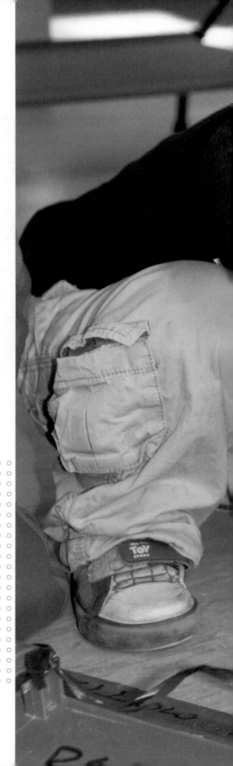

Reflecting on my practice

Jocelyn's key person Imran notices that she is showing more interest in climbing on things but is reluctant to go near the outdoor climbing trees. He talks with Dina, Jocelyn's Mum, at the end of the day and says he is puzzled about why, if Jocelyn is so interested in climbing, she would not like to play on the trees.

Dina says she is exasperated with Jocelyn at the moment because she is constantly climbing on the furniture. Imran asks Dina to come and look at the climbing tree area and see what she thinks. Dina is surprised that there are several different heights for the children to climb, ropes and handles to hold on to and lots of logs to balance on. She laughs a little and confesses to Imran that she had been telling Jocelyn not to climb or go near the trees because she might hurt herself and now she feels embarrassed. Imran laughs with her and invites her to stay a little while so that they can introduce Jocelyn to the climbing area together.

Imran talks with Dina about helping Jocelyn to gradually build her confidence by talking with her about the decisions she is making while climbing. When Jocelyn climbs on to a log, Imran says: "good thinking Jocelyn, your hands are holding on to keep you steady." After a few moments he says: "will you move a foot or a hand next?" Jocelyn puts her hand out to her Mum who holds it so that she has support to walk along the log.

- What opportunity do your parents have to explore your outdoor area and understand how you and the children are currently using it?

- What different scripts do you use with different children to prompt their own thinking and decision making when climbing?

- What risks are your parents currently worried about?

- In what ways are you working with them to explore the learning that will help the children be safe in the 'risky' situation?

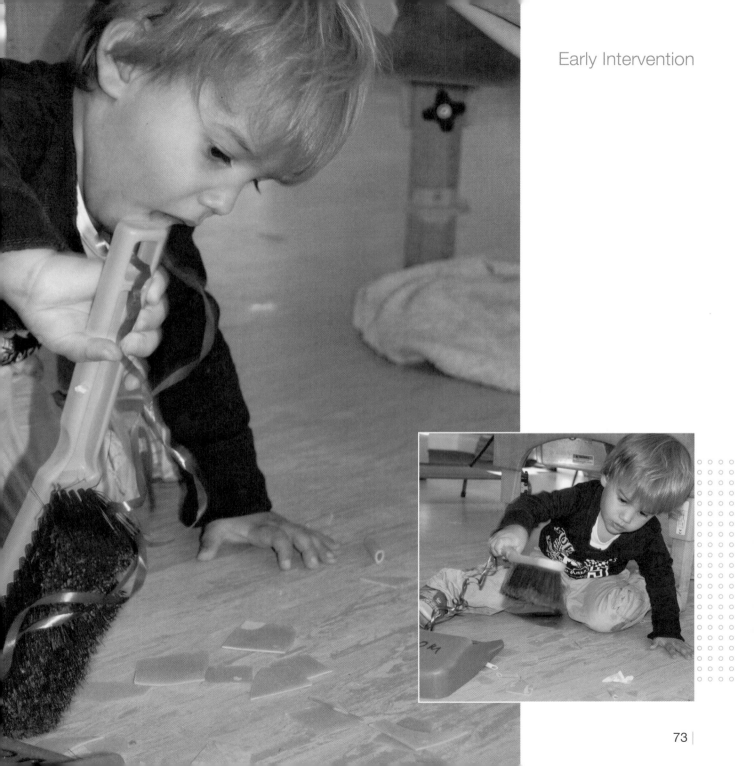

I am two!

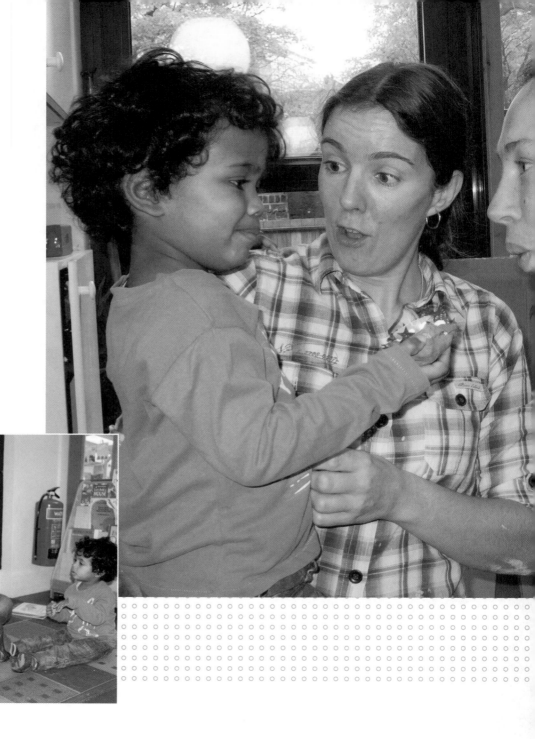

Chapter 8
Sharing

From day one

The very first contact between your setting and a parent will set the stage for the parents' views and attitudes towards those involved in the setting. This first contact may be with a member of staff whose main responsibility is administration or reception duties. So whilst your setting policy may have been developed and rigorously implemented with the staff team who are mainly engaged with children, others may not have been included in the process and be unclear about the ways in which their role and response can impact on relationships with parents.[59]

The process of developing effective communication with parents also involves being knowledgeable about local priorities and available support. Knowing your local area and the concerns and priorities local parents express is an important part of developing your team skills in engaging positively and sensitively with your current parents.[60] Each year there will be changes in the popularity and enthusiasm for different activities and events which you plan. It is always important to check with current parents the ways in which you can best offer support and engage them positively in the life of the setting.

A common issue is building realistic expectations of children's development, achievements and progress along with a shared understanding of them as individuals.

Seeing similar and different things

Each of us reacts in different ways to different situations and learning to do this appropriately can be a long and arduous process. Yet we are undoubtedly still the same person regardless of where we are and will therefore show similar aspects of ourselves where ever we find ourselves. The first few conversations between parents and practitioners can seem like you are not talking about the same child. This is not because either of you is making it up or over emphasising, more likely the child you are sharing feels very different in the setting compared to being at home. In the most familiar, usually their own home, they are likely to be more relaxed, confident and joyful about their engagement with their environment and the people around them. These characteristics of their learning will become increasingly obvious as they recognise and feel the familiarity of the setting. It is a huge step emotionally for two year olds to be in any place, no matter how lovely, without any of their 'special people.'

 Insights into a two year old's perspective:

These 'special people' or attachment figures are where, quite rightly as a two year old I go for comfort, security, reassurance, predictable responses. As practitioners you are ideally being added to my collection of people I trust who I feel will protect, nurture and be alongside me, especially when the world gets too exciting, frightening or just all wrong.[61]

As a parent this can feel strange, wanting these new adults to be a significant part of your child's life to care for them when you are not there. Parents may also be anxious that their child may prefers being with you rather than with them. As a practitioner it is a key part of your professional approach to develop the relationship with the parents based on them being the key attachment figures for the child and for you to be additional support for when the parents are not present. A particular time when two year olds can feel confusion and conflict about who is in charge and keeping them safe, is at the beginning and end of the day when parents and practitioners are present. It is important to talk through with parents how this might be played out before it happens. Even when a day has gone well, when the parent comes to collect the child, there can be an overwhelming relief and 'letting go' of emotions when the child sees the parent. This can include tears and a characteristic two year old 'splat' on the floor.

The danger of not talking through our thinking of why children may respond this way is that misunderstandings develop. In the example given, parents may worry that the professional practitioners will think that their child does not want to come home, or that they are frightened of the parent. Equally, misunderstandings on the part of the practitioner may include worrying that the parent thinks that the child has had a terrible day and has been upset and unhappy for most of it, with practitioners being unable to comfort them. Such a minefield of worry and anxiety can be avoided and understood so much better, if the adults are able to talk to each other, with the child's wellbeing central to their thinking and work out what is going on from the child's perspective.

Thinking about:
local resources for parents

- What is the range of agencies (health, social care, child and adolescent mental health (CAMHS), behaviour support, special educational needs and disabilities (SEND) services) represented at your local children's centres and offering support for parents?

- When you contacted your local Family Information Service how many of the local organisations which support parents did you already know about?

- Which of the local sources of support for parents have you contacted directly to explore ways in which they may be able to help your current parents?

- How many of your parents have spoken to you about useful support they have received locally? Are there other parents who may be interested in similar support?

Reflecting on my practice

Over the last week, Hamsa's key person, Nadhu, had noticed that Hamsa's Mum, Aleisha seemed to have a bit more time when she dropped Hamsa off in the morning. The evenings she found, were a rush and Aleisha rarely had time to hear about Hamsa's progress in the nursery.

The next morning Nadhu made a point of welcoming Aleisha when she arrived to drop Hamsa off at the nursery. Nadhu shared with Aleisha how well Hamsa was now using the potty and how pleased he was about his independence. Aleisha smiled and said she was pleased too although it didn't seem to be going as well at home.

Nadhu was surprised and asked if anything had changed in his routine. Aleisha looked worried. She explained to Nadhu that she was very worried about her teenage son who was having some problems. Aleisha told Nadhu that she was meeting with a group of Mums at the local children's centre, where there was a social worker specialising in working with teenagers who came to the sessions once a week.

Aleisha was worried though that Hamsa might be unsettled by the change in routine because rather than go home after nursery, he went to the crèche at the children's centre while she was at the group. Nadhu and Aleisha talked together about how to reassure Hamsa and agreed to talk again next week.

After hearing that the group was open to any local parents with concerns about their teenagers, Nadhu spoke Aleisha about her intention to approach the leader of the group to run a session in the nursery as well. Aleisha thought that this was a good idea and was happy for Nadhu to contact the leader of the group. Nadhu contacted the group leader and invited him to run a session for the nursery parents. He agreed, and the following month he ran a similar group at the nursery. Other local settings were informed and they encouraged other parents to attend as well.

Chapter 9
Acting

Taking action always sounds dramatic, important and irreversible but in reality most actions are small and at the time seem inconsequential. Consider the following example.

Parent: 'I'm surprised that Eddie has been trying to jump in a puddle with both feet at the same time. He's only two!'

Practitioner: 'What other physical things have you noticed recently that Eddie is able to do?'

In this scenario, the information is shared, the action is taken and the conversation begins. It may not all take place on one day and the parent and practitioner may both return to talk more about what they have noticed over several days on subsequent occasions, but it is the putting together of both adults views and their collective thoughts about the meaning of what has been noticed, which then indicates it is time to take the next step, often another small action as before.[62]

From a professional perspective keeping the topic of concern alive in conversation is just as important as listening carefully to the parents' ideas and thinking. Saying out loud and articulating clearly your concerns, helps to clarify thinking and the evidence on which the current hypothesis is based. Supervision discussions provide an ideal chance to talk through professionally what you are thinking and what you think you should do next to support the child and parent.[63]

Knowing the local context

Being a parent is an incredibly difficult job and all of us need support of some kind or another at some point. Just because you are technically a grown up and have a child, does not mean that you automatically know how to be a parent.

As early years practitioners we have regular and frequent contact with the children and their families so will gather some sense of how things are going for them. Having a two year old can be a real surprise for many families. As a parent you have nine months to prepare yourself for the arrival of the baby, but there are still many surprises as you get to know them as individuals. You realise that the authors of baby books might know a lot about babies in general, but know nothing about your baby! Just when you think you are getting the hang of how this parenting thing works, their language, thinking, understanding and physical abilities undergo a revolution and you hardly recognise the little person who is now your child. As a parent, and often also as a practitioner, working with two year olds can really make you question your own understanding and views about children.[64]

At this time of uncertainty and possible anxiety parents may appreciate some different kinds of support. It is really useful if you are aware and have up to date knowledge of local activities, groups and ways of accessing further help available to parents. These can range from drop ins or lunch clubs at the Children's Centre to Health Visitor, dietician or speech and language therapy sessions in different locations.[65] The Family Information Service in most local authorities is a good first point of contact to find out about what is available in your area. Local GP surgeries, libraries and schools can also be useful points of contact and sources of information about local provision. Although much reduced, many local authorities still have Early Years Teams to support practitioners.

The child's story

By the age of two children have a clear history of their development and progress from birth. Their story can be pieced together by information from parents about the pregnancy and birth, right through to the child's present fascinations and preoccupations. It is important that we maintain a perspective on how this child's story is unfolding and ensure that their needs are being met and wellbeing kept in focus.

As we have seen, growth and development should be rapid during these early years and any signs that this is not the case will give cause for concern. Supervision discussions give a useful opportunity to explore things you or the parents have noticed which are causing you concern. Working through the following set of questions can be a helpful way of clarifying what it is that is contributing to your concern. Seeking parents' views in the natural course of your daily, weekly and more formal conversations is crucial regardless of whether this is a shared concern, just theirs or just yours.

Bringing together parent and practitioner thinking

- What have I noticed?
- What have parents noticed?
- What do the parents think about their child's development?
- What evidence is there?
- What questions are there?
- Who might be able to contribute to our understanding?
- What would parents need to know first?
- What do parents need to know next?

If either you or parents have unresolved questions, then it is important to seek more information to deepen your understanding. As a step towards asking for help it is useful to work with parents to put together the key bits of information underlying the concern. Providing this for the person you decide to approach, gives them a good chance of recognising why there is a concern and to offer their expertise to best effect. Many services such as Health Visitors, GP practice nurses or social care now offer telephone advice lines, which can help to guide decision making and access to the appropriate support.

Safeguarding

As noted in the EYFS statutory guidance, children learn best when they are healthy, safe and secure and their individual needs are met and they have positive relationships with the adults caring for them. Therefore if current concerns constitute a safeguarding issue the setting named person should be informed and appropriate action taken in line with Local Safeguarding Children Board guidelines.

Although systems and proceedures are important it is ultimately individuals who protect children. It is essential that we are vigilant about safeguarding. Processes such as supervision, appraisal and performance management all combine to enable practitioners to update their knowledge, understanding and practice as well as having a forum to discuss concerns in depth.

A recent review of serious cases highlighted the importance of practitioners from different services being able to contribute key information as part of collaborative multi agency support for families. Parents are experts in their own experience and it is only by listening carefully that we can begin to appreciate some of their current pressures. They may well be struggling to deal with a range of issues such as financial problems, poor housing, bereavement, loss, illness, abuse, temporary or long term mental health issues, addiction, or relationship difficulties including domestic violence. In addition the parenting they received themselves may not have helped to equip them with the emotional and psychological resilience to be able to put their children's needs before their own in times of stress.

Practitioners in early years settings have a significant contribution to make to multi agency

collaboration, because of the amount of time spent with both the child and the parents often on a long term, daily basis. In particular, practitioners are able to give a chronology of the child's early years experience, including time at the current setting, other settings attended and progress to date in all areas of learning, including whether this is in line with typical development. Practitioners will also have a clear understanding of the child's regular carers and any significant changes in routines, hygiene or general wellbeing which are affecting the child.

The core understanding that will underpin multi-agency collaborative support for a child

and their family is that children's development will be affected by the circumstances in which they develop. Their development will be supported by good nutrition, good health, good hygiene and warm sensitive relationships including parents who are affectionate, emotionally available and accessible, and who are able to set developmentally appropriate boundaries and a context which provides physical and economic security.

Collaborative working

Recent reports and legislation from central government have in common the call for agencies involved with children and their families to work more closely together to provide coherent support. This is not necessarily about doing more but it is about doing things differently. Normally, our contact with other services would only be in response to a particular child or family. By making contact to explore how local services and support can be used and to share what we are doing, provides an opportunity for a different relationship. Over time, building on this first contact, we can engage with individuals and teams to make best use of our resources and skills. For example a local health visiting team may be focusing on healthy eating with a group of families in your area and a similar focus or information session may be useful for your parents. The Health Visitor may be able to combine this visit with some two year reviews for parents who would find it difficult to attend clinic appointments.

Ongoing discussions can put in context the different ways in which we review children's progress given our different levels of involvement over time. These discussions can help to challenge our thinking about the messages and support parents are getting and to identify ways to make this more coherent for them. A core part of this process is giving other teams 'good press' with parents. Practitioners can help by making genuinely positive comments about the services on offer, the staff involved as well as the support parents can expect. If we have concerns about any aspects of another service, these need to be taken directly to the teams involved. The resulting discussion offers opportuntities to share ideas to improve mutual understanding.

Conclusion

And finally…

This book set out to explore the characteristics of 'twoness' and to give some insights and reflections about the transformational processes which occur around this time in a child's life. By the time a child is two they already have their own unique set of experiences that contribute to their story. Our two year olds also have a network of adults who are helping them to understand 'how the world works.' They have relationships with other children and a range of adults that are also all unique. The characteristics of these relationships and the circumstances that they are living in all contribute to their unique perspective and understanding.

In the context of the EYFS in England, the principles and approaches provide an environment that can nurture each unique child's competencies and exploration of their world. A child's EYFS experience will only contribute to giving them a positive start in life if it is of high quality. Undoubtedly, there will always be a range of quality and expertise demonstrated in our early years settings, but if the ethos we create is one where as individuals we are striving to deepen our understanding, build our knowledge base and increase our professional skills, we will be able to give each child the 'best possible chance' for a positive experience.

With the current government initiative in England to offer funding for two year olds in our settings we have an opportunity to reflect on our practice and ensure it is tailored to the needs of our two year olds and their families. Recognising and understanding the challenges which families may be facing, the ways in which we can both offer support and signpost other local services can make a significant difference to the child's experiences. As practitioners, this can feel like a daunting task at times but it is important to remember that high quality provision is characterised by positive and supportive interactions. If we focus on ensuring that each interaction that we are engaged in, whether with the child or adult, is open, positive, building confidence and developing a respectful relationship, then we will create a strong basis for continuing to improve the quality of our provision.

From its very conception life is a lottery; the vulnerability of the developing baby, the experience of childbirth and the circumstances into which the child is born are many and varied and all have an influence. Being two is a time of transformation in thinking, understanding, autonomy and independence. While it can be confusing for the child, it can also be a complex time for the adults caring for them. Being a source of sensitive, reliable and knowledgeable support is an important part of our role as practitioners. Most importantly though, being with two year olds is fun and full of excitement, if we choose to engage with them in that way.

I am two!

Resources

Useful publications

Department for Education (2012). *Early intervention Grant and free early education places for disadvantaged two-year-olds FAQs*. Available online from **www.education.gov.uk**

Department for Education (2011). *Support and aspiration: A new approach to special educational needs and disability - A consultation*. London: Department for Education. Available online from **www.education.gov.uk**

Department for Education (2011). *Supporting Families in the Foundation Years*. London: Department for Education. Available online from **www.education.gov.uk**

Department of Health (2012). *Healthy Child Programme: pregnancy and the first five years of life*. London: Department of Health. Available online from **www.dh.gov.uk**

Department of Health (2010). *The Pregnancy Book 2009*. Available online from **www.dh.gov.uk**

Early Education (2012). *Development Matters*. London: Early Education. Available online from **www.foundationyears.org.uk**

JABADAO (2009). *Developmental Movement Play: Final Report and Recommendations from a 10-year action research project investigating the way the early years sector supports the youngest children to be fully physical*. Leeds: JABADAO Available online from **www.jabadao.org**

Learning and Teaching Scotland (2010). *Pre-Birth to Three: Positive Outcomes for Scotland's Children and Families. National Guidance*. Scottish Government.

Moylett, H. & Stewart, N. (2012). *Understanding the Revised EYFS*. London: Early Education.

National Childminding Association (2012). *EYFS and You*. London: NCMA

National Children's Bureau (2012). *A Know How Guide - The EYFS progress check at age two*. London: NCB. Available online from **www.foundationyears.org.uk**

National Children's Bureau (2010). *Early Support - Information for parents*. London: DCSF. Available online from **www.ncb.org.uk**

Ofsted (2011). *Good Practice Local Safeguarding Children Boards*. Manchester: Ofsted. Available online from **www.ofsted.gov.uk**

Royal College of Paediatrics & Child Health (2009). *Personal Child Health Record*. South Shields: Harlow Printing Limited. Available online from **www.rcpch.ac.uk/PCHR**

Scottish Government (2009). *Curriculum for Excellence: Experiences and Outcomes for all curriculum areas*. Edinburgh.

Stewart, N. (2011). *How Children Learn. The characteristics of effective early learning*. London: Early Education.

Welsh Assembly Government (2008). *Foundation Phase Framework for Children's Learning for 3 to 7-year-olds in Wales.*

Welsh Government (2012). *Flying Start. Strategic Guidance.* Crown Copyright.

Legislation

Department for Education (2011). *The Education Act 2011*. London: Department for Education. Available online from **www.education.gov.uk**

Department for Education (2012). *The Early Years Foundation Stage*. London: Department for Education. Available online from **www.education.gov.uk**

Department of Health (2012). Health and Social Care Act 2012. London: Department of Health. Available online from **www.dh.gov.uk**

Useful websites

Brain Facts **www.brainfacts.org**

Centre for Excellence and Outcomes in Children and Young People's Service **www.c4eo.org.uk**

Child Poverty Action Group **www.cpag.org.uk**

Contact a Family **www.cafamily.org**

Department for Education **www.education.gov.uk**

Department of Health **www.dh.gov.uk**

Early Education **www.early-education.org.uk**

Education and Resources for Improving Childhood Continence **www.eric.org.uk**

Education Scotland **www.educationscotland.gov.uk**

Foundation Years **www.foundationyears.org.uk**

Jabadao **www.jabadao.org**

Learning through Landscapes **www.ltl.org.uk**

National Children's Bureau **www.ncb.org.uk**

NHS Choices **www.nhs.uk**

Ofsted **www.ofsted.gov.uk**

Relate **www.relate.org.uk**

Royal College of Paediatrics and Child Health **www.rcpch.ac.uk**

Welsh Assembly Government **www.wales.gov.uk**

I am two!

The balance wheel can be a useful visual tool to prompt discussions about how a child is spending their time either across a day or a week. It can be used to think about the amount of time they spend inside or outside, with key adults at home or in the setting, time asleep or awake. It can be especially helpful to use before and after a change in routine or strategies, to see what the impact might have been. For example, for a two year old who is very energetic and difficult for parents to engage positively with at home, discovering that they are only having two hours of their week

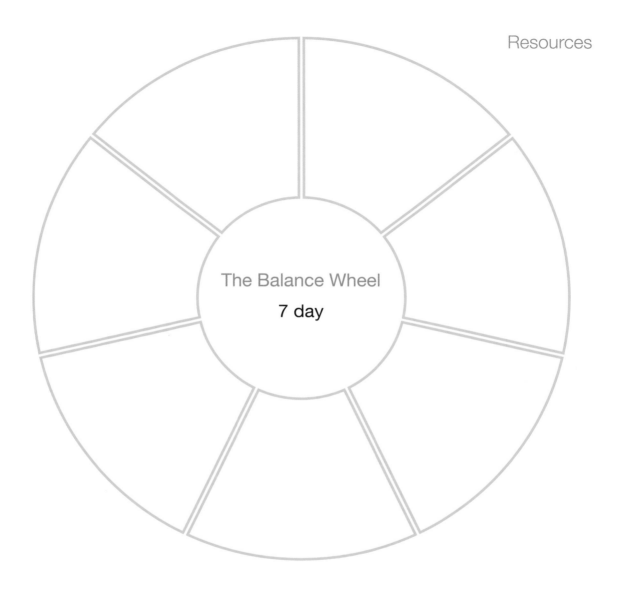

The Balance Wheel

7 day

outside might lead to finding ways of increasing this with a visit to the park on the way home or at weekends. The differences in responses at home can then be compared.

Other variations on the timescale can easily be devised to suit the situation. The visual simplicity helps to make it accessible for all and easy to manage with only a few notes and a date needed to explain the context.

Are we thinking the same things?

Use the prompts below to share what you are thinking about your two year old.
It can be reflected on after six months or a year to see if things look the same.

What does a good day look like for your 2 year old?

- At home

- At nursery

- What does a good week look like?

- What do you hope life will be like when your two year old is:
    - 5 years old
    - 7 years old
    - 10 years old
    - 16 years old
    - 25 years old

- At the moment, I notice that _____ is
    - motivated by
    - most engaged in
    - demonstrating her thinking by

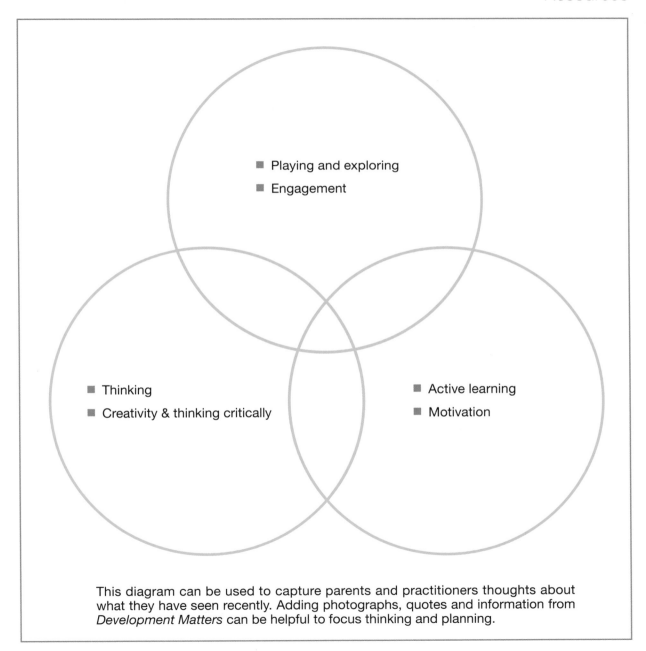

Playing and exploring
■ Engagement

■ Thinking
■ Creativity & thinking critically

■ Active learning
■ Motivation

This diagram can be used to capture parents and practitioners thoughts about what they have seen recently. Adding photographs, quotes and information from *Development Matters* can be helpful to focus thinking and planning.

References

[1] OECD (2011). *Doing Better for Families*. OECD Publishing.

[2] Melhuish, E., Belsky, J. & Barnes, J. (2010). Evaluation and Value of Sure Start. *Archives of Disease in Childhood*, 95/3, pp.159-61.

[3] Allen, G. (ed.) (2011). *Early Intervention: The Next Steps.* London: Cabinet Office.

[4] Bird, S. & Rogers, M. (2010). *Early Intervention for Children and Families,* London: C4EO.

[5] Hirsch, D. (2008). *Estimating the Costs of Child Poverty*. York: JRF.

[6] Easton, C. & Gee, G. (2012). Early *Intervention: informing local practice* (LGA Research Report). Slough: NFER.

[7] Wood, D., Bruner, J.S. & Ross, G. (1976). The role of tutoring in problem solving. *Journal of Child Psychology and Psychiatry*, Vol. 17, pp. 89-100.

[8] Department of Health (2009). *Birth to Five*. London: Department of Health. p 65.

[9] Garrett, B. (2009). *Brain and Behaviour*. London: Sage Publications. p 344.

[10] Shonkoff, J.P. & Phillips, A. (eds) (2000). *From Neurons to Neighbourhoods*. Washington: National Academy Press. pp. 47-50.

[11] Evangelou, M., Sylva, K., Kyriacou, M., Wild, M., & Glenny, G. (2009). *Early Years Learning and Development: Literature Review.* London: Department for Children, Schools and Families.

[12] Evangelou, M., Sylva, K., Kyriacou, M., Wild, M., & Glenny, G. (2009). *Early Years Learning and Development: Literature Review.* London: Department for Children, Schools and Families. p 71.

[13] DeCasper, A. & Spence, M. in Ward, J., (2012). *The Students Guide to Social Neuroscience.* London: Psychology Press.

[14] Evangelou, M., Sylva, K., Kyriacou, M., Wild, M., & Glenny, G. (2009). *Early Years Learning and Development: Literature Review.* London: Department for Children, Schools and Families. p. 65-71.

[15] Brownell, C.A & Kopp, C.B. (eds) (2007). *Socioemotional Development in the Toddler Years: Transitions and Transformations.* New York: The Guildford Press. p 10.

[16] Oates, J., Karmiloff-Smith, A. & Johnson, M.H. (eds) (2012). *Early Childhood in Focus 7: Developing Brains.* Milton Keynes: The Open University Press. p 16.

[17] Oates, J., Karmiloff-Smith, A. & Johnson, M.H. (eds) (2012). *Early Childhood in Focus 7: Developing Brains.* Milton Keynes: The Open University Press., p 26.

[18] Gerhardt, S. (2004). *Why love matters.* Hove: Routledge. p 24.

[19] Society for Neuroscience (SfN) (2012). *Brain facts: A Primer on the Brain and Nervous Systems.* Washington: Society for Neuroscience. p 17.

[20] Rogoff, B. (2003). *The Cultural Nature of Human Development*. Oxford: Oxford University Press. p 68.

[21] Fernyhough, C. (2008). *The Baby in the Mirror.* London: Granta Publications. p 15.

[22] Shonkoff, J.P. & Phillips, A. (eds) (2000). *From Neurons to Neighbourhoods.* Washington: National Academy Press. p 55.

[23] Shonkoff, J.P. & Phillips, A. (eds) (2000). *From Neurons to Neighbourhoods*. Washington: National Academy Press. p 93.

[24] Rogoff, B. (2003). *The Cultural Nature of Human Development*. Oxford: Oxford University Press. p 64.

[25] Ward, J. (2010). *The Students Guide to Cognitive Neuroscience.* Hove: Psychology Press. p 264.

26 Hughes, C. (2011). *Social Understanding and Social Lives*. London: Psychology Press. p 17.

27 Gerhardt, S. (2004). *Why love matters*. Hove: Routledge. p 25.

28 Carpendale, J. & Lewis, C. (2006). *How Children Develop Social Understanding.* Oxford: Blackwell Publishing.

29 Hughes, C. (2011). *Social Understanding and Social Lives*. London: Psychology Press. p 37.

30 Rogoff, B. (2003). *The Cultural Nature of Human Development*. Oxford: Oxford University Press. pp. 111-117.

31 Robinson, M. (2003). *Birth to One*. Buckingham: Open University Press. p 50.

32 Oates, J. (ed) (2010). *Early Childhood in Focus: Supporting Parenting*. Milton Keynes: Open University Press.

33 Dorman, C. & Dorman, H. (2002). *The Social Toddler.* Surrey: CP Publishing. p 136.

34 Rogoff, B. (2003). *The Cultural Nature of Human Development*. Oxford: Oxford University Press. p 4.

35 Brooker, L. & Woodhead, M. (eds) (2008). *Early Childhood in Focus: Developing Positive Identities*. Milton Keynes: Open University Press. p 4.

36 Brooker, L. & Woodhead, M. (eds) (2008). *Early Childhood in Focus: Developing Positive Identities*. Milton Keynes: Open University Press. p 26.

37 Vandenbroeck, M., Roets, G. & Snoeck, A. (2009). Immigrant mothers crossing borders: Nomadic identities and multiple belongings in early childhood education. *European Early Childhood Education Research Journal* 17(2). p 48.

38 Schaffer, H.R. (1996). *Social Development.* Oxford: Blackwell Publishing. p 119.

39 Oates, J., Karmiloff-Smith, A. & Johnson, M.H. (eds) (2012). *Early Childhood in Focus 7: Developing Brains.* Milton Keynes: The Open University Press. p 30.

40 Meins, E., Fernyhough, C., Wainwright, R., Gupta, M.D., Fradley, E., & Tuckey, M. (2002). Maternal mind-mindedness and attachment security as predictors of theory of mind understanding. *Child Development*, 73, pp. 1715—1726.

41 Oates, J., Karmiloff-Smith, A. & Johnson, M.H. (eds) (2012). *Early Childhood in Focus 7: Developing Brains.* Milton Keynes: The Open University Press. pp. 4-12.

42 Hughes, C. (2011). *Social Understanding and Social Lives*. London: Psychology Press. p 33.

43 Brownell, C.A & Kopp, C.B. (eds) (2007). *Socioemotional Development in the Toddler Years: Transitions and Transformations.* New York: The Guildford Press. p 149.

44 Brownell, C.A & Kopp, C.B. (eds) (2007). *Socioemotional Development in the Toddler Years: Transitions and Transformations.* New York: The Guildford Press. p 66.

45 Rogoff, B. (2003). *The Cultural Nature of Human Development*. Oxford: Oxford University Press. p 18.

46 Ward, J. (2012). *The Students Guide to Social Neuroscience.* Hove: Psychology Press. p 77.

47 Brownell, C.A & Kopp, C.B. (eds) (2007). *Socioemotional Development in the Toddler Years: Transitions and Transformations.* New York: The Guildford Press. p 294.

48 Brownell, C.A & Kopp, C.B. (eds) (2007). *Socioemotional Development in the Toddler Years: Transitions and Transformations.* New York: The Guildford Press. p 222.

49 Nelson, K. (2007). Becoming a Language User — Entering a Symbolic World in Brownell, C.A & Kopp, C.B. (eds) *Socioemotional Development in the Toddler Years: Transitions and Transformations.* New York: The Guildford Press. p 233.

50 Evangelou, M., Sylva, K., Kyriacou, M., Wild, M., & Glenny, G. (2009). *Early Years Learning and Development: Literature Review.* London: Department for Children, Schools and Families.

51 Evangelou, M., Sylva, K., Kyriacou, M., Wild, M., & Glenny, G. (2009). *Early Years Learning and Development: Literature Review.* London: Department for Children, Schools and Families.

52 The Scottish Government (2012). *Bringing up Children: Your Views.* Edinburgh: Scottish Government

53 Royal College of Paediatrics & Child Health (2009). *Personal Child Health Record.* South Shields: Harlow Printing Limited. Available online from **www.rcpch.ac.uk/PCHR.**

54 Stewart, N. (2011). *How Children Learn: The characteristics of effective early learning.* London: Early Education.

55 UNICEF (2001). *Early Childhood Development: The Key to a full and productive life.* New York: UNICEF.

56 Allen, G. (ed.) (2011). *Early Intervention: The Next Steps.* London: Cabinet Office.

57 Dowling, M. (2005). *Young Children's Personal, Social and Emotional Development* (2nd Ed). London: Paul Chapman Publishing. p 64.

58 Brownell, C.A & Kopp, C.B. (eds) (2007). *Socioemotional Development in the Toddler Years: Transitions and Transformations.* New York: The Guildford Press. pp. 67-99.

59 Elfer, P., Goldschmied, E., Selleck, D.Y. (2012). *Key Persons in the Early Years: Building Relationships for quality provision in early years settings and primary schools.* London: Routledge.

60 Roberts, K., (2009). *Early Home Learning Matters: A Good Practice Guide.* London: Family and Parenting Institute.

61 Elfer, P., Goldschmied, E., Selleck, D.Y. (2012). *Key Persons in the Early Years: Building Relationships for quality provision in early years settings and primary schools.* London: Routledge. Chapter 2.

62 Mathieson, K. (2005). *Social Skills in the Early Years.* London: Paul Chapman Publishing.

63 Mathieson, K. (2007). *Identifying Special Needs in the Early Years.* London: Paul Chapman Publishing.

64 Wall, K. (2006). *Special Needs and Early Years.* London: Paul Chapman Publishing.

65 Nutbrown, C. & Clough, P. (2006). *Inclusion in the Early Years.* London: Sage Publications.

Bibliography

Allen, G. (ed.) (2011). *Early Intervention: The Next Steps*. London: Cabinet Office.

Bird, S. & Rogers, M. (2010). *Early Intervention for Children and Families*. London: C4EO.

Brooker, L. & Woodhead, M. (eds) (2008). *Early Childhood in Focus: Developing Positive Identities*. Milton Keynes: Open University Press.

Brownell, C.A & Kopp, C.B. (eds) (2007). *Socioemotional Development in the Toddler Years: Transitions and Transformations*. New York: The Guildford Press.

Carpendale, J. & Lewis, C. (2006). *How Children Develop Social Understanding.* Oxford: Blackwell Publishing.

DeCasper, A. & Spence, M. in Ward, J., (2010). *The Students Guide to Social Neuroscience*. London: Psychology Press.

Department for Education (2011). *The Education Act 2011.* London: Department for Education. Available online from **www.education.gov.uk**

Department for Education (2011). *Support and aspiration: A new approach to special educational needs and disability - A consultation*. London: Department for Education. Available online from **www.education.gov.uk**

Department for Education (2011). *Supporting Families in the Foundation Years.* London: Department for Education. Available online from **www.education.org.uk**

Department for Education (2012). *Statutory Framework for the Early Years Foundation Stage: setting the standards for learning, development and care for children from birth to five.* London: Department for Education. Available online from **www.education.org.uk**

Department for Education (2012). *Early intervention Grant and free early education places for disadvantaged two-year-olds FAQs*. Available online from **www.education.gov.uk**

Department of Health (2009). *Birth to Five.* London: Department of Health.

Department of Health (2009). *The Pregnancy Book 2009.* Available online from **www.dh.gov.uk**

Department of Health (2012). *Health and Social Care Act 2012.* London: Department of Health. Available online from **www.dh.gov.uk**

Department of Health (2012). *Healthy Child Programme: pregnancy and the first five years of life.* London: Department of Health. Available online from **www.dh.gov.uk**

Dorman, C. & Dorman, H. (2002). *The Social Toddler*. Surrey: CP Publishing.

Dowling, M. (2005). *Young Children's Personal, Social and Emotional Development* (2nd Ed). London: Paul Chapman Publishing.

Early Education (2012). *Development Matters.* London: Early Education. Available online from **www.foundationyears.org.uk**

Easton, C. & Gee, G. (2012). *Early Intervention: informing local practice (LGA Research Report).* Slough: NFER.

Elfer, P., Goldschmied, E., Selleck, D.Y. (2012). *Key Persons in the Early Years: Building Relationships for quality provision in early years settings and primary schools*. London: Routledge.

Evangelou, M., Sylva, K., Kyriacou, M., Wild, M., & Glenny, G. (2009). *Early Years Learning and Development: Literature Review*. London: Department for Children, Schools and Families.

Fernyhough, C. (2008). *The Baby in the Mirror*. London: Granta Publications.

Garrett, B. (2009). *Brain and Behaviour*. London: Sage Publications.

Gerhardt, S. (2004). *Why love matters*. Hove: Routledge.

Hirsch, D. (2008). *Estimating the Costs of Child Poverty*. York: JRF.

Hughes, C. (2011). *Social Understanding and Social Lives*. London: Psychology Press.

JABADAO (2009). *Developmental Movement Play: Final Report and Recommendations from a 10-year action research project investigating the way the early years sector supports the youngest children to be fully physical*. Leeds: JABADAO Available online from **www.jabadao.org**

Learning and Teaching Scotland (2010). *Pre-Birth to Three: Positive Outcomes for Scotland's Children and Families. National Guidance*. Scottish Government.

Mathieson, K. (2005). *Social Skills in the Early Years*. London: Paul Chapman Publishing.

Mathieson, K. (2007). *Identifying Special Needs in the Early Years*. London: Paul Chapman Publishing.

Meins, E., Fernyhough, C., Wainwright, R., Gupta, M.D., Fradley, E. & Tuckey, M. (2002). Maternal mind-mindedness and attachment security as predictors of theory of mind understanding. *Child Development*, 73, 1715—1726.

Melhuish, E., Belsky, J. & Barnes, J. (2010). Evaluation and Value of Sure Start. *Archives of Disease in Childhood*, 95/3, pp. 159-61.

Moylett, H. & Stewart, N. (2012). *Understanding the Revised EYFS*. London: Early Education.

National Childminding Association (2012). *EYFS and You*. London: NCMA.

National Children's Bureau (2010). *Early Support - Information for parents*. London: DCSF. Available online from **www.ncb.org.uk**

National Children's Bureau (2012). *A Know How Guide - The EYFS progress check at age two*. London: NCB. Available online from **www. foundationyears.org.uk**

Nelson, K. (2007). *Becoming a Language User – Entering a Symbolic World* in Brownell, C.A & Kopp, C.B. (eds) *Socioemotional Development in the Toddler Years: Transitions and Transformations*. New York: The Guildford Press.

Nutbrown, C., & Clough, P. (2006). *Inclusion in the Early Years*. London: Sage Publications.

Oates, J. (ed) (2010). *Early Childhood in Focus: Supporting Parenting*. Milton Keynes: Open University Press.

Oates, J., Karmiloff-Smith, A. & Johnson, M.H. (eds) (2012). *Early Childhood in Focus 7: Developing Brains*. Milton Keynes: The Open University Press.

OECD (2011). *Doing Better for Families*. OECD Publishing.

Ofsted (2011). *Good Practice Local Safeguarding Children Boards*. Manchester: Ofsted. Available online from **www.ofsted.gov.uk**

Roberts, K., (2009). *Early Home Learning Matters: A Good Practice Guide*. Family and Parenting Institute.

Robinson, M. (2003). *Birth to One*. Buckingham: Open University Press.

Rogoff, B. (2003). *The Cultural Nature of Human Development*. Oxford: Oxford University Press.

Rosen, M. (1989). *We're Going On A Bear Hunt*. London: Walker

Royal College of Paediatrics & Child Health (2009). *Personal Child Health Record*. South Shields: Harlow Printing Limited. Available online from **www.rcpch.ac.uk/PCHR**

Scottish Government and COSLA (2008). *The Early Years Framework.* Edinburgh.

Scottish Government (2009). *Curriculum for Excellence: Experiences and Outcomes for all curriculum areas.* Edinburgh.

Scottish Government (2012). *Bringing up Children: Your Views*. Edinburgh.

Schaffer, H.R. (1996). *Social Development*. Oxford: Blackwell Publishing.

Shonkoff, J.P. & Phillips, A. (eds) (2000). *From Neurons to Neighbourhoods*. Washington: National Academy Press.

Society for Neuroscience (SfN) (2012). *Brain facts: A Primer on the Brain and Nervous Systems*, Washington: Society for Neuroscience.

Stewart, N. (2011). *How Children Learn: The characteristics of effective early learning*. London: Early Education.

UNICEF (2001). *Early Childhood Development: The Key to a full and productive life.* New York: UNICEF.

Vandenbroeck, M., Roets, G. & Snoeck, A. (2009). Immigrant mothers crossing borders: Nomadic identities and multiple belongings in early childhood education. *European Early Childhood Education Research Journal* 17(2).

Wall, K. (2006). *Special Needs and Early Years*. London: Paul Chapman Publishing.

Ward, J. (2010). *The Students Guide to Cognitive Neuroscience*. Hove: Psychology Press.

Ward, J. (2012). *The Students Guide to Social Neuroscience*. Hove: Psychology Press.

Welsh Assembly Government (2008). *Foundation Phase Framework for Children's Learning for 3 to 7-year-olds in Wales.*

Welsh Government (2012). *Flying Start. Strategic Guidance.* Crown Copyright.

Wittgenstein, L. (1953). *Philosophical Investigations*. New York: Macmillan.

Wood, D., Bruner, J.S. & Ross, G. (1976). The role of tutoring in problem solving. *Journal of Child Psychology and Psychiatry,* Vol. 17, pp. 89-100

Index

About the authour

Kay has worked in early years and primary education since 1981 supporting children with additional needs and their families. She previously led the Early Years Inclusion Team in the London Borough of Croydon and was a National Strategies Early Years Regional Advisor.

Kay's main areas of interest are, improving the quality of adult/child interactions, developing adult problem solving approaches to SEN and behaviour issues. Her specific interest in children's social, emotional and behavioural learning has also led to her focussing on the development of social competence in young children as part of her PhD research at University of Sussex. Her doctorate was awarded in 2011.

Kay is an *Associate* of Early Education.

About Early Education

Early Education was founded in 1923. Ninety years later we continue to remain committed to supporting families and the professional development of all those working in early childhood education to ensure effective early childhood education experiences of the highest quality for all children in the United Kingdom.

Through our work, we support both strategically and practically, those working across early childhood education. We endeavour to effect change and respond rapidly to the changes in the early childhood education policy and practice landscape through consultation, campaigning and dialogue with policy makers as well as practically through projects, publications and resources, training and professional development and information and advice.

For more information about our work visit **www.early-education.org.uk**

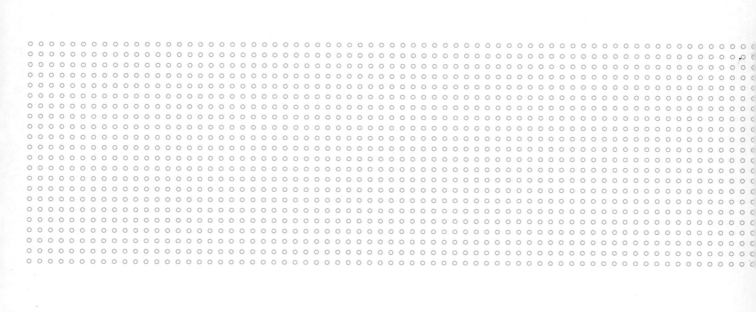